FAITH TEST

Marla Jones

Table of Contents
Introduction

Chapter 1   3
The Battle
If God is real, why does all this stuff happen to me?

Chapter 2   17
Cloudy Days
Why does God allow suffering?
My Battle.

Chapter 3   36
Becoming a Warrior
I can't see a way out.
Where do I start?

Chapter 4   51
The Warrior Within
I'm my own worst enemy.

Chapter 5   61
The State of the Heart
This God Stuff Doesn't Seem To Work For Me.

Chapter 6   72
Covenant or Contract
Christianity is just a bunch of rules, isn't it?

Chapter 7   84
Covenants of the Bible
So what's following God look like?

Chapter 8   99
Hearing from God
Does God really speak to people?

Chapter 9 — 110
Listen!
Why am I not hearing anything?

Chapter 10 — 117
What I Heard
What does God say when He speaks?

Chapter 11 — 134
Healing
Does God still heal people?

Chapter 12 — 146
A journey in healing
How does God heal people?

Chapter 13 — 158
Grow up!
Why do Christians seem like such hypocrites?

Chapter 14 — 176
Fear Factor
What are you afraid of?

Chapter 15 — 207
It's not about the Money
Why does the church always ask for money?

Chapter 16 — 220
Can I get a Witness?
Do I have to be a door knocker?

Conclusion

Discussion Questions — 1

Dedication

This book is dedicated to all who search for the true answers to life. For Jesus promises "For everyone who asks receives, he who seeks finds and to him who knocks, the door will be opened."

I am so grateful for my husband, Mark; you have always been there for me when I need you the most.

To my beautiful children, Elijah, Trinity, Ethan and Benjamin, I pray you will know Jesus personally as you journey through life's mountains and valleys. He will always be there for you. He will never leave you nor forsake you. Nothing can pluck you from the palm of His hand.

I am so grateful to those who have inspired me to write and have helped in the production of this book. A special thank you to Susan, Bea, Katherine, Lloyd, Ryan, Tim, Liz, Christine, Joanna, Peter, Rob, Kirsten, Doug and Scott. To my church family, thank you for your daily example of giving, loving and serving others.

Cover art- Thank you to Nicole and Corrine.

Jesus did many other things as well.
If every one of them were written down,
I suppose that even the whole world would not have room for the books that would be written.   John 21:25

Introduction

So often we let our questions and doubts about God get in the way of really experiencing God. Some people reason that if they don't understand God, then surely He doesn't exist. Others may think that He's not interested or doesn't care, causing them to doubt or question their faith. Our human reasoning often blocks us from seeing or experiencing God. Predetermined mindsets don't give God much of a chance to show his true character to us. If anyone mentions God or religion, walls go up within our minds and our hearts. It looks a little bit like: "If there was a God, then why...?"

This is not a Christians vs. non-Christian thing. Even Christians struggle with doubts and wonder why they aren't hearing from God or experiencing Him in the way they desire. Some try to hide it or justify it, but the truth is that no one person has all of the answers. God, however, does.

We tend to be afraid to ask questions or have conversations about our doubts because either we will offend someone or someone will want to convert us to their version of religion. The answer? Just don't talk about it at all. Yet conversations are crucial to understanding each other, our purpose in life and who God really is. This is what this book is: a conversation or at least the start of one.

I've taken some of the tough issues, the unmentionables of this so-called, "Christianity" and brought them to the forefront so that we can have an honest look at the issues that may be stopping you from experiencing God in amazing ways. God wants to answer your questions. He delights in revealing His wisdom and knowledge. He is not altered in the least by your questions, anger, doubts, struggles and that "S" word so often thrown around, SIN. He loves you. Why let that stuff stop you from finding God? God is not what you expect. He's amazing!

When you begin to get to know God for yourself, you'll be blown away by what He has in store for you. You'll know it's God because, in all of your wildest dreams, you could never imagine what He is about to say to you. He holds the answers you are looking for.

This book is designed to get you to look at things from a different perspective, to get you thinking outside of what you have been taught by culture, tradition, education or media influence. My hope is that, whether you already believe in God or not, this book will open your heart and free your mind from the blocks that have been frozen in place so there will be a sliver of an opening for God to come in and rock your world.

Just so you know, God has been waiting for you and no matter what your thoughts are about Him, He will continue to wait for you. He knew you would pick this book up, so why not read it and see what insights you might find about God within its pages.

Chapter 1
The Battle
If God is real, why does all this stuff happen to me?

*Who is this King of glory?
The Lord strong and mighty, the Lord mighty in battle.*
Psalm 24:8

Do you ever have days where everything seems stacked against you? If you're at all like me maybe I should say, "Is there ever a day when everything isn't stacked against you?"

The other day was pretty much like most days for me. It just played out differently. I woke up late. I was in such a deep sleep that when I sat up, I had a crick in my neck. I hate that feeling because I know that it takes a couple of days and a couple of visits to the chiropractor to work it out. I thought to myself, "I'll have a couple of aspirin and a hot shower to loosen up the muscles."

Unfortunately, it wasn't until I was standing under the showerhead that the cool water reminded me of the power outage we had the previous day. Our hot water system is on a timer, so it was during this short, contemplative moment that I realized we hadn't reset the timer. After my moment of enlightenment, I quickly jumped out and got dressed so I could warm up again. (Just for the record, I still forgot to set the timer for the hot water and was just as surprised the following day.)
I then decided that one of my super shakes was in order for a healthy start to the day. I had a feeling I was going to need it. I

loaded up the blender with berries, freshly squeezed orange and beetroot juice, spirulina powder and a bit of flaxseed oil. It was at the exact moment that I pressed the start button that I realized I hadn't tightened the bottom of my blender enough, so the dark red pulpy juice started to leak all over the cream-colored counter and onto the floor. I knew that I was in a no-win situation because if I lifted the blender to tighten the bottom, it would all come crashing out. Yet if I left it like it was, it would only delay the inevitable.

Later that same day, I was relaxing on the couch, enjoying the quiet state of the house, when I realized it was a WEDNESDAY, which meant it was a half-day for my child at Kindergarten. I was half an hour late picking him up and felt like "Mom of the Year" when I approached the room to find him sitting with his bag in the corner of the room, which was empty apart from two teachers with the "How could you forget your child?" look all over their faces.

I wish I could say this was a one-off example, but stuff like this happens to me all of the time! I have, for the most part, accepted this as just part of life, my life. Even as I write this, I am laughing to myself as a memory comes to mind of a time when I was in the school parking lot. I was trying to get my baby stroller out of the trunk of my car. It was quite bulky and heavy. So I was pulling with all of my might when the stroller just seemed to launch itself out of the car. It came out so quickly and with such force that I knocked my head on the bolt where you connect the baby seat. I hit the bolt with such tremendous power that as I fell backward, I knocked myself out.

I awoke about a minute or so later lying on the gravel road with the stroller on top of me, just staring at the clouds rolling by in the sky above and a throbbing headache. Sad but true. Not many have this sort of claim to fame.

Thankfully, after a bit of time has passed, these stories make me and others laugh.

Now I get that a lot of this is caused simply by being the graceful doe that I am. I have a loaded brain crammed with too much information, a tendency to forget the most important information and amidst the hurry of life, an inner drive to get as much done as possible in the least amount of time. Yet on a deeper level, it seems like there is more.

On the surface, these things can be quite funny yet they're also disturbingly annoying. They could be chalked up to random coincidence perhaps. But when it goes to the next level, when serious life problems hit, the humor stops. When things seem to hunt me down, latch on and not let go, it no longer feels so random but somehow planned.

It is at these times in particular that I tend to think of a battle. I guess it's because of what I've heard many war veterans say about real battles; in that often you don't clearly see who or what you are fighting, but you do know that you are at war. You're not sure what will happen next or how you will deal with it. You struggle and wrestle with the problems. You turn the problem over and over in your mind trying to find solutions. You wonder how you will survive, questioning, "Why is this happening to me?"

It is often in these times of hardship that people will think about God, if only to say, "If there is a God, why would He let this happen to me?" or "Where is God?"

These kinds of battles are hard to talk about. They are personal, leaving the feeling of being trapped and alone. They are never "fair". They leave you so gutted and vulnerable that you just don't know what to do. Sometimes it's just like being pelted over and over again. Every time you get up, something comes against you and knocks you over again. Other times, it's as if you are in a nightmare, unable to wake up or get out of it. You struggle on as if you were going up a hill made of thick molasses. Each step is a strain and even though you are working so hard to move forward, you find that you keep sliding back.

I have sat with friends as they have experienced shocking life experiences. A fire that has destroyed both property and home, a family going through bankruptcy, a child with a life-threatening disease, a child that died at birth, an accident claiming lives yet leaving others with damaged bodies and horrible memories.

These experiences have not only caused hurt and agony but have left scars.

"My mother died when I was 12, leaving me to an abusive and drunk father and no one to help me? Where was God then?"

"I lost the use of my leg from the accident. I can no longer run and play with my kids. Was that part of God's plan?"

"Outward" battles are things that just happen to us. We have no control over the situations. The "outward" battles involve things that rob us of "life". We are not dead, yet we don't quite feel alive either. The outer battles don't physically kill us but they stop us from living the kind of life we deserve, a life of freedom, joy and happiness. The way we instinctively know life is meant to be.

Some of my battles have included financial struggles, broken relationships, family members with medical and mental illnesses, jaw reconstruction surgery, an eating disorder, a car accident, anxiety, some very strange illnesses and a couple of near-death experiences. Although I breeze over these hardships now, trust me when I say that I understand what it means to suffer. I did nothing wrong. These things just happened to me. They happen to everyone, just in different ways. They frustrate our hopes and dreams. We don't ask for them nor deserve them but there they are. And will continue to be. Situations will happen to us that are out of our control.

There are many stories of suffering in the Bible. So this is not something new or unknown to God. My challenge to you is to find someone in the Bible who didn't suffer. Details of various stories are recorded for a reason. God knows that every human being will suffer in some way and He knows we will wrestle with that suffering, even to the point of blaming Him. So why does He continue to let suffering exist? It is within Biblical stories that we begin to find our answers.

Let's take a look at just one example recorded in the Bible of a man who suffered unjustly probably more than anyone on the face of the earth. His name is Job (yep that's his name although it's pronounced Jōbe). This guy went through more than I could ever imagine.

Job was a good man. In fact, he was better than a good man. The Bible records the Lord saying of Job, "*There is no one on earth like him; he is blameless and upright, a man who fears God and shuns evil.*"

There was no one else on earth, not one other person, who was as blameless and upright as Job. I think he was a Biblical giant, up there with Abraham and Elijah.

Then one day, out of the blue, this happened:

> *A messenger came to Job and said, 'the oxen were plowing and the donkeys were grazing nearby, and the Sabeans attacked and carried them off. They put the servants to the sword, and I am the only one who has escaped to tell you!'*
>
> *While he was still speaking, another messenger came and said, 'The fire from God fell from the heavens and burned up the sheep and the servants ...'*
>
> *While he was still speaking, another messenger came and said, 'The Chaldeans formed three raiding parties and swept down on your camels and made off with them. They put the servants to the sword ...'*
>
> *While he was still speaking, yet another messenger came and said, 'Your sons and daughters were feasting and drinking wine at your brother's house, when suddenly a mighty wind swept in from the desert and struck the four corners of the house. It collapsed on them and they are dead.' Job 1:14-19*

Now that is a bad day. Let's try and bring it into modern times.

Imagine you're sitting in your office at work one day and you get a phone call from the fire department. They tell you that your house and all the contents have spontaneously combusted from a gas pipe bursting and then catching alight. The house has been completely burnt to the ground. And of all days, you left your car in the garage at home because it was "Bike to work" day.

You are trying to deal with the news when investigators come into your office. Apparently, the shares you invested in, unbeknownst to you, were for an illegal company. You have just lost all of your life's savings.

While you are still dealing with the fire department on the phone, a colleague runs into your office and says what he has just seen on the news. A flight has just gone down, crashing into the ocean. The impact was so forceful that everyone on the plane has died. He asks, "Wasn't your family flying today?"

Horror sinks to your stomach as you realize it was the same flight that your four children, their spouses and your grandchildren had taken to come home for the Christmas holidays.

That is unimaginable, yet it was the reality for Job. And that's not all! Let's skip to the next chapter:

> *So Satan went out from the presence of the Lord and afflicted Job with painful sores from the soles of his feet to the crown of his head. Then Job took a piece of broken pottery and scraped himself with it as he sat among the ashes.*

> *His wife said to him, 'Are you still maintaining your integrity? Curse God and die!'*
>
> *He replied, 'You are talking like a foolish woman. Shall we accept good from God, and not trouble?'* Job 2:7-10

Now Job has some sort of infection of boils all over his body! How much can a person take? Can you imagine what would be going through Job's mind? I'm guessing that if you have suffered in any way you most likely can guess what was going through his mind. I'm sure he was questioning, "What happened? Where are you, God?"

He probably wondered whether or not he also was about to die or even worse, be left with a nagging wife who instead of offering support, starts an argument with him.

If you look at the previous verses, Job did not do anything to cause these things to happen. When they do happen, amazingly, Job maintains his integrity and refuses to blame or curse God.

It would be easy to get caught up in the awful details of the story and leave it at that, however, when we look beyond the story of Job, we begin to see that there is another story being told. There is another realm introduced to us, a spiritual realm. This is a realm that most of us don't feel comfortable talking about but a realm that exists nonetheless.

It is in this realm we see someone who lays quite low, as quiet as a snake, come forward. An angelic being who attempted to be his own god rather than follow the one true God.

> *Then Satan went out from the presence of the Lord.*
> *Job 1:12*

I have come to understand that as humans, we only get glimpses into the vast spiritual realm that surrounds us. In those glimpses, we just don't get the full understanding. I think God does this mainly for our protection. But He allows just enough information to get through to bring to light some very important aspects of this realm.

Let's look into what happened in the spiritual realm of this story.

> *One day the angels came to present themselves before the Lord, and Satan also came with them. The Lord said to Satan, 'Where have you come from?'*
>
> *Satan answered the Lord, 'From roaming throughout the earth, going back and forth on it.'*
>
> *Then the Lord said to Satan, 'Have you considered my servant Job? There is no one on earth like him; he is blameless and upright, a man who fears God and shuns evil.'*
>
> *'Does Job fear for nothing?' Satan replied. 'Have you not put a hedge around him and his household and everything he has? You have blessed the work of his hands, so that his flocks and herds are spread throughout the land. But now stretch out your hand and strike everything he has, and he will surely curse you to your face.'*

The Lord said to Satan, 'Very well, then, everything he has is in your power, but on the man himself do not lay a finger.'

Then Satan went out from the presence of the Lord.
Job 1:6-12

Now before we instinctively jump to any conclusions, let's take a moment to review what may not initially stand out in this passage.

Satan is not happy. I'm pretty sure he never is. In the original Hebrew text, Satan's name means: 'the accuser', 'the enemy', 'the trouble-maker' 'adversary'. Anyways, he's ticked at God because God has put a hedge of protection around Job and has blessed everything Job has put his hands upon. Satan can't touch Job unless God allows him to. Not only that, God controls exactly how much Satan can interfere with Job's life.

Satan wants God to strike everything that Job has to prove that Job will curse God. That seems to be the only reason. Think about that for a minute. There is only one reason Satan wants to strike us, yet there are thousands of reasons why the Lord would allow it.

I find it interesting that in this passage God seemingly can't or won't strike Job. I believe this says a lot about who He is. It is not His character to simply hurt without cause. He allows Satan to strike everything that Job has but puts a boundary around Job. Even as Satan approaches God again for another try in the second chapter of Job, God still does not allow Satan to touch Job's life.

As you read these passages, you begin to get a real sense that God is not worried about Satan going out to strike Job with everything he's got. God is not worried because He knows Satan, He created him. Contrary to many people's perceptions, Satan does not sit on the other side of God in a giant battle of who is greater.

Have a close look at Job 1:6-12 and you will see the following:

> *Angels are under the authority of God.*
>
> *Satan is an angel created by God who chose to disobey and suffered the consequences.*
>
> *Satan is not a threat to God, nor is he equal in power. Satan answers to the Lord.*
>
> *There is no good found in Satan.*
>
> *God knows what Satan will do before he does it.*
> *God is not worried or frightened by the things Satan has in store for us.*
>
> *Even Satan has boundaries, again showing God's ultimate control over everything.*
> *God has a purpose and a plan for our suffering.*
>
> *And we know that in all things God works for the good of those who love him, who have been called according to his purpose.*
> *Romans 8:28*

In Chapters 3-38 you will read about a conversation between Job and his three closest friends. It is too long to print here but so worth the reading.

In summary, Job's friends tried to give him advice. It was the kind of advice that really didn't help Job but at least they stuck by him trying to help. It seems in the midst of suffering, people often come out of the woodwork to help "fix" you. Job's friends thought that Job had done something to offend God because let's face it, who gets hit like that unless they are cursed in some way?

But in all of this, Job remains righteous. Yes, he questions God but he never curses Him. He was righteous before, during and after this time of suffering.

Just like Job's friends, we can also tend to assume, in our view of theology, that God always rewards good and punishes evil, with no apparent exceptions allowed. That if we follow God, He will never allow anything we deem bad to happen to us. We find it hard to accept that there are things that God does which will never fit into our compartmentalized understanding. This leaves little room for understanding the mystery and divinity of God's ability to use and direct suffering in such a way that it actually helps us; it can be hard for us to even imagine suffering can be something other than punishment.
This says to me that God sees suffering in a completely different way than what we do. Whether we like it or not, we only have a very limited view of what suffering is all about. God sees the whole picture.

As you read the book of Job, you see many aspects of the battle Job had to fight. He battled with physical pain and the shock of having lost everything he held dear. He battled the comments and opinions of his wife, his close friends and his community. He even fought battles in the realms of his mind. He questioned and had some very dark times. Who wouldn't in the same circumstances?

When we read to the end of this story we find a better-than-we-could-have-ever-hoped-for happy ending. Job 42:7-16, gives us some more valuable insights:

We will never fully understand someone else's suffering. It really is between that person and God.

Suffering is for a time.

It is okay to question God, in fact, He may just answer!
Job refused to blame God and held onto his faith. When Job's battle was over, he spoke with God directly and received a clear revelation from God. He saw things that very few men ever saw. God honored him.

The Lord restored his health. The Lord restored his fortunes and gave him twice as much as he had before.

The Lord blessed the latter part of Job's life more than the former. He had seven sons and three daughters. After this, Job lived a hundred and forty years, seeing his children and grandchildren to the fourth generation. He died an old man, full of years. Who knows what followed as he went into that spiritual realm after death? Was he reunited for eternity with those he had lost previously?

What Satan takes away, God can miraculously restore in ways beyond our comprehension.

Suffering is part of life, everyone's life. If it hasn't come already, it's on its way. Suffering, difficulties, hardships, trials come in a variety of forms but none of them feel pleasant. The Bible warns us of suffering, shares stories of suffering, teaches and helps us with suffering. Jesus spoke about it often. The only thing He spoke about more is His love for us and how we should love others.

It has taken me a long time to come to a point where I am beginning to accept that suffering is not just "bad". There's a lot more to suffering. I don't like suffering. Like most people, I get mad, angry, blame others and question God. I have fallen to my knees and wept. I've had times I just wanted to die and times when I was just afraid. Yet when I have allowed God into that suffering with me, instead of fighting Him, I began to experience God's presence, power and love for me. There is something crucial to our suffering and hardships in the spiritual realm.

Suffering gets to the core of who we are and sometimes we don't like what we see. Suffering is not God testing who we are but God allowing us to see what we are made of. It is a way to demonstrate our faith. To exercise what God has instilled within us.

Chapter 2
Cloudy Days
Why does God allow suffering?

...so that no one would be unsettled by these trials. For you know quite well that we are destined for them.
1 Thessalonians 3:3

Yesterday, I was taking clothes off of the clothesline because some dark clouds were slowly rolling in and it looked as if there was a good chance of rain. My nine-year-old daughter was watching me while sitting on her swing. She finally said to me, "You know that as soon as you get all those clothes inside, it's not gonna rain anymore?"

"Yep", I replied. "But if I leave them up there,"

"It's gonna rain," she finished my sentence.

"Why is that Mom? Why is it that when you want something to happen, it doesn't and when you don't want something to happen, it does?"

I laughed to myself and thought, "Good question!"

She's only at the start of her life and has already experienced some of the frustrations of everyday living. I thought to myself, "Oh Honey if you only knew the road that lay ahead. It's part of life. We either laugh about it and move on, or it'll just get the better of us."

There is good and bad in every aspect of life. That's a given. I'm forever telling my children this and follow it up by saying, "Try and look for the good, but be aware of the bad".

Although my son only sees the good in his computer games, I have to point out to him that he is missing out on some real-life adventures. Although my daughter may only see the bad in having to do chores, I remind her how good it feels to have a clean house.

I know this is very simplistic but I learn a lot from my kids. Even though the situations change over time, as adults we can forget to see that there really is good and bad in every situation and it is good to see both sides.

Focusing on the good gives us pleasure and can lead our heart to a state of gratitude. It is in this state of gratitude that we begin to find contentment in life. Knowing there is good even when we don't see it, gives us hope when we find ourselves in a dark place. But keeping in mind that there is a bad side to everything, helps us realize there are limits and boundaries that are better left uncrossed. Being aware of the bad can prepare us so that we don't get caught out by our own weaknesses. Without the bad, you would never fully understand or appreciate the good.

When we are going through a particularly bad time in our life it can be hard to see any good. We hurt and we question, "Why?" Many times it feels as if our world is shattered and we are left wondering how we can go on. For many, bad times can go on for a long time, often hidden away so that no one else even knows we are suffering. But God does know and He sees into the most hidden recesses of our hearts. Knowing this can lead us to question, "If God sees what is happening to me, why doesn't He stop it or make it go away?"

This same question can be worded in many ways.

"Did God create the bad and does God cause bad things to happen?"
"Does God send things to hurt me or punish me?"

"Why did God allow something (horrible) to happen?"

"If He's in control of everything, why are so many people suffering and starving in the world?"

If left unanswered, these questions will slowly begin to cause us to doubt and undermine what we do know is true of God.

Basically, it comes down to questioning the very nature or character of God. These are very loaded and deep questions and there isn't one simple answer. It is my hope that as you read this chapter, you will take everything before God in prayer and seek Him for your own understanding.

To start, I want to look at God's character. Read the following verses aloud to yourself:

> *For I am the Lord your God who takes hold of your right hand and says to you, Do not fear; I will help you.* Isaiah 41:13
> (As I read this, I envision a Father standing alongside his child, offering support and a loving touch.)

> *The Lord is close to the brokenhearted and saves those who are crushed in spirit. The righteous person may have many troubles, but the Lord delivers him from them all;* Psalm 34:18-19

> *The salvation of the righteous comes from the Lord; He is their stronghold in times of trouble.* Psalm 37:39

> *And so we know and rely on the love God has for us. God is love. Whoever lives in love lives in God, and God in them.* 1 John 4:16
> *Cast all your anxiety on him because he cares for you.* 1 Peter 5:7

Let's go back to the very beginning of time just after God created humans.

> *The Lord God took the man and put him in the Garden of Eden to work it and take care of it. And the Lord God commanded the*

> man, 'You are free to eat from any tree in the garden; but you must not eat from the tree of the knowledge of good and evil, for when you eat from it you will certainly die.' Genesis 2:15-17

God didn't have to put the tree of the knowledge of good and evil in the garden. But by doing so He gave Adam and Eve a choice. He knew it was the only way to offer real life and real love.

We live in an age of amazing technology and inventions. We even have phones that talk to us and carry out specific commands! We are surrounded by some of the greatest inventions ever made, yet while they will wow you and stun you, they will never do more than their creator has designed them to do. You will never be able to have a real relationship with anything you create because you are not God!

And don't try and tell me that you created your children because, if you stop to think about it, you did very little in that process! If you want to know how in-depth God is, just look closely at the structure of the human body; how all those molecules, brain cells and blood cells work alongside the miracle of a heart that beats all on its own. The point is, only God can bring life out of nothing and place His image within it.

But God has done an amazing thing! He has designed His creation in such a way that He really can have a relationship with the created. How? He has given us the gift of choice. We can choose either to turn away from God, which saddens His heart, or we can choose to enter into that relationship with Him. You can't make someone love you, but if someone chooses out of their own will to love you, how beautiful and special is that?

If God seems too distant and too big to grasp the concept of love, look at the character of Jesus, God in the flesh. Jesus is the mirror image of God the Father in heaven. Jesus lived to show us a reflection of God. Jesus described Himself as a shepherd, not just an average shepherd who looks after his sheep, but the kind of shepherd who would lay down His life to save his sheep. Which, He did, in the end when He died upon the cross.

If you observe the life of Jesus, you will notice that he went from town to town, teaching and speaking about God so that people could begin to understand God's love for them. But He didn't just tell stories; He showed the Father's love by healing people and caring for them. He didn't hurt people. No, He was about the only one who would dare to talk to, touch and minister to the outcasts of society, those whom no one else would go near. He wanted all people to know that they were loved by God. He loved like no other man has ever loved.

You might say to yourself, "Yeah, but that was Jesus and God is different." Yet listen to the very words of Jesus,

> My sheep listen to my voice; I know them, and they follow me. I give them eternal life, and they shall never perish; no one will snatch them out of my hand. My Father, who has given them to me, is greater than all; no one can snatch them out of my Father's hand. I and the Father are one. John 10:27-30

Again Jesus expresses this very clearly when we listen in on his conversation with Philip in John 14, starting at verse 6. Come, let's listen in:

Jesus: I am the way and the truth and the life. No one comes to the Father except through me. If you really know me, you will know my Father as well. From now on, you do know Him and have seen Him.

Philip: Lord, show us the Father and that will be enough for us.
Jesus: Don't you know me, Philip, even after I have been among you such a long time? Anyone who has seen me has seen the Father. How can you say, 'Show us the Father?' Don't you believe that I am in the Father, and the Father is in me? The words I say to you I do not speak

on my own authority. Rather, it is the Father, living in me, who is doing his work. Believe me when I say that I am in the Father and the Father is in me; or at least believe on the evidence of the works themselves.

He goes on to give a compelling description of the relationship between Jesus, God, the Holy Spirit and those who choose to follow. People often refer to this as the "Trinity": God, Jesus and Holy Spirit. Imagine as Jesus invites us into this Holy Communion.

Jesus: Very truly I tell you, whoever believes in me will do the works I have been doing, and they will do even greater things than these, because I am going to the Father. And I will do whatever you ask in my name, so that the Father may be glorified in the Son...
And I will ask the Father, and he will give you another advocate to help you and be with you forever- the Spirit of truth.

God's ultimate goal in sending His son Jesus was to make a way for His creation, who ran away with the free choice options and have made generations of bad choices. He sent Jesus to save us. We see this in one of the most well-read verses in the Bible:

> For God so loved the world that he gave His one and only Son, that whoever believes in Him shall not perish but have eternal life. For God did not send His Son into the world to condemn the world, but to save the world through Him. John 3:16-17

This is the heart of God. If God has put so much effort into creating us, calling us, wooing us into a relationship with Him, why would He cause bad things to randomly happen to us? Yet the passage does not end there.

> *Whoever believes in Him is not condemned, but whoever does not believe stands condemned already because they have not believed in the name of God's one and only Son.* John 3:18

Now to the one who stands condemned, is that condemnation coming from God or from a choice they have made to stand outside of God on their own?

> *This is the verdict: Light has come into the world, but people loved darkness instead of light because their deeds were evil. Everyone who does evil hates the light, and will not come into the light for fear that their deeds will be exposed.* John 3:19-20

There is definitely a choice to be made here. How can the person who chooses to stand outside of the authority and realm of God, judge God for doing bad things? It seems the perspective is completely wrong if you are trying to measure up life outside the one who created the scales.

Sometimes it is so hard to see things when our perspective is so out of whack. We have to remember we are human, finite and weak beings compared to God who is all-knowing, all-powerful and eternal. The more I get to know of God, the more my perspective changes. I think to myself, "Ah-ha, I get it. I understand what you are teaching God", only to find I have gathered a drop in the sea of His wisdom.

I love collecting quips and quotes, especially ones that expand my perspective about God and life. There is one quote I have kept for years because it teaches me that I have a very limited perspective on life. It says:

"Have you ever wanted to ask God why He allows poverty and hunger to exist when He could do something about it?"
It then goes on to say:

"What if He asks you the same question?"

I thought to myself, "Here I have been questioning and judging God while quite blissfully remaining unaware of my responsibility in living life on this planet."

If you need a refresher on how limited our perspective is, just visit a local high school and talk to teenagers about what is important in life, visit a retirement center and ask what is wrong with our world or chat with my five-year-old about ownership of toys in general. You'll see very quickly that our perspective is limited by so many factors like education, culture, isolation, opinion and humanity, just to mention a few.

What you may see as a bad thing may be seen very differently in the eyes of God. Going back to the previous example, if we didn't have needy people in our lives, how would we learn to share, to love others and show compassion?

Ok, that's all understandable, but how do you explain something as terrible as September 11 and other atrocities currently happening around the world? Quite simply, I don't. I don't try to explain things so horrific and evil as terrorism, war, merciless killing and other acts of cruelty. Who could? That is evil in its purest form. But I do know that is definitely not God. That is what it looks like when man completely turns away from the conscience and moral truth that God created within us at birth. God does not cause evil because there is no evil in him. When I look at the intricacy of the delicate flower petals or the birth of a baby, I see the fingerprint of God. No, evil does not look the same.

We do have an enemy and we would be naive to ignore the reality of Satan and his demonic realm. He is very subtle and deceiving.
Yet, we don't have to look far to find that evil also exists within each of us. Any thought, mindset or opinion that is not subject to God has evil. Although I don't know nor want to know exactly how Satan works, I do know that he was in the garden of Eden and was the initiator of the first choice to turn away from God. Adam and Eve chose to listen to Satan rather than to God and as a result, made bad choices on their own without any help. Yes, Satan can

play a part in the equation but we do a great job of messing things up on our very own.

If you were to take every aspect of God out of a person all you would be left with is pure evil. As horrible a thought as it is, we are all capable of such evil. As hard as it may be to accept, terrorists believe they are doing the right thing. They have been trained and taught to do such evil. Who is to say we would be any different if we were trained and taught since birth to do evil? To God, evil is evil. He calls it for what it is. There is no ratio of one evil being worse than another. In God's eyes, it is all the same. Evil is when we make a choice to follow our way over God's way and we are all guilty. This is why we are in desperate need of a savior.

Yet even within such horrific acts of evil we see evidence of love breaking through. Acts of bravery, courage, love and justice can be seen within those who died trying to save others. I believe the spirit of God ministers to all who are in trouble and call on His name. I believe He gave comfort to those in need and continues to do so today. And someday, I do believe God will bring to account every human being, Christian and non-Christian, and righteous justice will be given.

Ok, let's bring it down to a personal level. What about trials in our own lives? Does God use affliction to discipline His people? My answer might surprise you, for I believe the answer is yes. I do believe God allows affliction along with the consequences of our sin for training and refining. He uses these struggles to mature and refine people, especially those He loves.

> *It was good for me to be afflicted so that I might learn your decrees. The law from your mouth is more precious to me than thousands of pieces of silver and gold. Your hands made me and formed me; give me understanding to learn your commands. May those who fear you rejoice when they see me, for I have put my hope in your word. I know, Lord, that your laws are*

righteous, and that in faithfulness you have afflicted me.
Psalm 119:71-75

The word, "Afflict" means to cause pain or suffering, to affect, to trouble or knock down.

From my research, I discovered several words mean "Afflict" in Latin. Two seem to strike a chord with what is written in this psalm.

Adficio, which means: to affect, weaken, sap, exhaust, drain.

And the word, *Macto* - one definition is: to magnify, glorify, honor

Unfortunately, most people need to be in a place where they have exhausted all of their own energy, used up all of their own ideas and have become weak before they will turn to the Lord for help. It is in this state of being, when there is nothing of us left, that we tend to turn to God for answers and search for God. It is here that most will begin a relationship with God. When we ask Him to become our Lord, He will be magnified, even glorified, in our life. When we are weak (*Adficio*), He is glorified (*Macto*). We also will be honored (*Macto*) simply because He lives within us. People will see Christ in us, which is why we are called "Christian".

God is available 24/7, all the time. He would rather you come to know Him in your happy times when all is well in life and you are feeling good. Unfortunately, it seems to be the condition of mankind that we want to do our own thing and will only seek God when we need help.

If that is the only way God will have the chance to begin a relationship with you then He will encourage that route to come quickly so as to not miss out on a moment with you. He is after all a great Father and wants you to know Him better. Yet, affliction is used for so much more than initially drawing you to God.

> *Our fathers disciplined us for a little while as they thought best; but God disciplines us for our good, that we may share in his holiness.* Hebrews 12:10

Do I believe God disciplines us? You bet. The Bible is full of examples of God disciplining His children. But remember the root word of discipline is to disciple. Jesus called only twelve disciples to be the closest to him. He taught them through the life experiences they shared together. He wants the same for us. He wants you to be His disciple.

> *For he does not willingly bring affliction or grief to the children of men.* Lamentations 3:33

Occasionally, I have had to step back and allow pain to teach my child a lesson rather than me stepping in to save him again. Did I enjoy it? No, but that was the only way that child would change his destructive behavior. This is often called, "tough love". Sometimes continually bailing your child out can do more harm than good.

When you have many little personalities in the household, discipline looks different for each child. For one child, sending her to her room (isolation) is the most painful discipline. For another child, taking away a favorite toy seems so severe. Whereas for another child, physical pain caused by their own foolishness, is the only thing that seems to brings a positive response. Each child is very different. If I dished out the same discipline for all of them, it just wouldn't work. If I tried isolating all of my children, some would just happily play with the toys in their room. It certainly wouldn't teach them to think about their behavior!

Yet, if I didn't discipline them at all, my children would be just like the many problem children (and adults) we see today, hurting others and their property without feeling any remorse at all. Look at your actions. If there were no police around, would you stick to the speed limit? If you weren't required by law to report your income and pay taxes, would you willingly give money to the government out of concern for your country? Laws and enforcement of those laws teach us to do the right things for ourselves and for those who live around us.

> *Say to them, 'As surely as I live, declares the Sovereign LORD, I take no pleasure in the death of the wicked, but rather that they turn from their ways and live. Turn! Turn from your evil ways! Why will you die, O house of Israel?' Ezekiel 33:11*

I do not think that God enjoys disciplining or allowing affliction upon His children. What does He enjoy? He enjoys watching his creation find freedom and life as it is designed to be. Does a surgeon enjoy the process of cutting, removing and stitching? Possibly, but I think a surgeon finds more satisfaction with the end result of a healthy person and having been part of the process of healing.

God shows mercy willingly but sends affliction out of absolute necessity. He knows the end result of our sin and what it can do to us if left unchecked. He desires that everyone would enter a relationship with Him for eternity, but evil will not be allowed to cross the line into eternity. Evil and all those who choose to follow it rather than God will, in the end, face eternal death. Which is the other definition of Afflict- *Macto*: to slay, fight, punish.

Read the following passage to see how God is like a Father, grieving over His children's bad choices and how He determines to show them mercy again and again. He so desires them to choose life over death.

> *My people are determined to turn from me. Even though they call me God Most High, I will by no means exalt them.*
>
> *"How can I give you up, Ephraim? How can I hand you over, Israel? How can I treat you like Admah? How can I make you like Zeboyim?*

> *My heart is changed within me; all my compassion is aroused.*
> *I will not carry out my fierce anger, nor will I*
> *devastate Ephraim again. For I am God, and not a man—the*
> *Holy One among you. I will not come against their cities. Hosea*
> *11:7- 9*

Affliction is simply a means to an end. Affliction brings maturity, wisdom and humility in people. Affliction from God is refining. It causes us to be better people. He does it in love, for our benefit. It should not be seen as some random terrible sentence.

Affliction weans us from this world and its temporary sufferings and turns us to an eternal God.

God promises to be close to us during these times of disciplining and teaching. He is not only close to us in our times of affliction, His spirit moves within our very soul. He comforts the afflicted.

> *Shout for joy, O heavens; rejoice, O earth; burst into song, O*
> *mountains! For the LORD comforts his people and will have*
> *compassion on his afflicted ones.*
> *Isaiah 49:13*

We all experience discipline so you are not alone in your times of affliction. However, your discipline may look different than others, as I have already touched upon. I mention this so that we are careful not to judge others in their times of affliction. You do not know what God is doing in the life of another even if you have gone through something similar in your own life. Certainly pray with your brother or sister as they go through these times of affliction and encourage them that God loves them, but don't preach or assume that they are sinning. Job's friends got a severe reprimand from God when they took that route. You can read about that in the book of Job, chapter 42.

But take courage in times of affliction; God disciplines those He loves and there is much to learn in our times of affliction. God does not afflict for affliction's sake. It is for a specific purpose. His ultimate goal is to bring freedom into your life.

When we have a cancer within our body, it needs to be removed. Most likely, that will involve pain. But in physical terms, we willingly endure pain if in the end it brings life. In the spiritual, it is the same. Sometimes God needs to remove a cancerous attitude or a sinful nature in our life to bring us healing.

> *For he wounds, but he also binds up; he injures, but his hands also heal. Job 5:18*

As a surgeon has to cut (or "wound the skin") to get to the cancer and ("injure" the surrounding tissue) to take the cancer out, he is in the very process of healing. He wounds to heal. Can you understand this concept?

God is an amazing surgeon. His light shines on the very heart of the problem. He knows exactly what needs to be removed to fix the problem. He is concise and direct. He does not waste any opportunity. The process only takes longer if we are slow to cooperate with Him. His hope is that we will be quick to repent and change. However, if we do not choose to be quick, He will not give up on us. My goal these days is to learn my lessons quickly. I do not want to keep going through the same trials over and over again!

> *And the God of all grace, who called you to his eternal glory in Christ, after you have suffered a little while, will himself restore you and make you strong, firm and steadfast. To him be the power forever and ever. Amen.*
>
> 1 Peter 5:10-11

The good news is that your suffering will end and the Creator who loves you will make you whole, even better than you were before! Hold onto Him in your time of need and He will never disappoint. He will bring you peace that goes beyond all of human understanding in the very midst of your trials and affliction.

> *The Almighty is beyond our reach and exalted in power; in his justice and great righteousness, he does not oppress. Job 37:23*

There is a difference between affliction and oppression. God is never oppressive to His people. Affliction, as hard as it may be, is bearable and causes us to grow. Oppression is from the enemy and is mixed with our own sin. Yet, the answer is the same for both; it is only in the power of God we will overcome.

God designed life to be good. Then good was given a choice. When the choice was made to turn away from God and go a separate way, evil entered in. Did God design the evil? No. Does God allow evil to exist? Yes, for a time and within boundaries, so that true relationship may exist between God and His creation. And He always allows for a way out of evil and into His eternal care.

Once evil entered the world the more complex life became. Evil is like drops of food coloring put into water. The more the liquids are mixed, the more entwined the color becomes and depending on how much is put in, it touches different parts of the water in various ways. But It's only a matter of time before the color blends in so well that you can't remember what the original water looked like.

We don't know where evil and its temptation will surface, but we have a choice to let God deal with it or try and deal with it ourselves. Have you ever tried to pull food coloring out of a mixture? It's impossible. Hence our frustration in life. We fool ourselves into believing we can make things right in our lives, but only He who made the original mix is capable of making things right again.

Are you wondering where to even start to try and get to know God for yourself?

If you have never done so before, take the time to look up passages in the Bible that describe the character of God. Get to know God from His own words found in the Bible. If you have a paper version, you could use the concordance in the back of your Bible or you could simply Google "the character of God- Bible." There are several Bible apps and various Bibles online, all of which have search bars and various versions to make reading the Bible easier than ever.

If perhaps, you were feeling a bit bolder, you could go to a local church or a Christian gathering and speak to other Christians. Ask them what God has done in their lives. Question them as to what made them want to become a Christian. Listen to their stories of amazing encounters with God.

God is a keeper of His word and Jesus specifically challenges us to not be shy but search for Him and He will reveal Himself to us.

> *Ask and it will be given to you; seek and you will find; knock and the door will be opened to you.* Matthew 7:7

My Battle.

Like many kids in their high school years, I had a tough time trying to "fit in". My job at the local ice-cream parlor didn't help my dream to look like the many skinny, beautiful girls I would see at school. I struggled with pimples, fashion sense, permed hair, limited brain skills in most subjects and ever-present low self-esteem.

The size of my school was overwhelming with 726 students in my Grade 9 class and nearly 29,000 kids combined Grades 9 to 12. I simply got lost in the system. So lost that when they sent me the class photo at the end of the year, I went to find my picture and it wasn't even there! What a letdown!

The only benefit of being lost in a system is that it makes it harder for the system to keep track of students when they are not at school. Although my skills may not have earned me many "A+"s on my report card, they excelled in ways getting out of school and making it look like I was there. Why go to a place that continually reminds you what a failure you are?

I had a lot of acquaintances at school but no close friends. I struggled with constantly feeling alone. My parents were divorced so my Dad was never around. My Mom worked full time so I rarely saw her either.

There was something else I felt I couldn't share with anyone; I struggled with evil forces that were hard to explain. I had nightmares nearly every night. I saw things in my room that scared me. I had a mind that rivaled Stephen King. I could always see the dark side of things. I wanted someone to help me but there didn't seem to be anyone I could trust.

I looked into every religion I could find but something kept pulling me back to the God of the Bible. I prayed but I didn't hear any answers or feel any presence. I remember clearly one night as I sat at my bedroom window and cried out, "God if you are there, then prove you exist!" I was tired of living in a nightmare all alone. I fell asleep crying.

The next day I managed to get to school but on the way home something very unusual happened. I got on the bus and looked towards the back. Two girls were sitting at the back waving at me and asking me to sit with them. I didn't recognize them so I turned around to see if they were talking to someone behind me but no one was there. So I went back to sit with them.

I found out they were sisters that had just recently moved to the area. They hadn't met many people and wanted to know if I could come to their house after school.

Well to make a long and intricate story a bit shorter, these girls were Christians. Over time, we became the best of friends. They answered hundreds of questions, debated issues on faith and prayed for me. Through them, I discovered God and decided to become a Christian. After becoming a Christian, life didn't become easier, it became lighter.

It wasn't easier because I still had to go to school, my parents were still divorced and I had many difficulties I had to endure. It became lighter because now I knew I didn't have to travel this journey alone anymore. Now I had someone that actually could understand and help me. By depending on God and making the time to learn from Him, I was beginning to get the skills to handle the problems I faced and I had this strength within me that I had never experienced before. It was a supernatural strength from God downloaded into me. It was a never-ending supply of power ready for me anytime I needed to draw from it. So life became lighter. I want to emphasize the fact that the hardships did not stop when I became a Christian. Some of the hardest things I would ever experience in life were yet to come.

It was shortly after becoming a Christian that I developed an eating disorder that I struggled with for years. I can't even put to words how difficult that journey was yet I learned things about myself and about God that helped me to get through. Eventually, this led to a miracle healing, a divine revelation from God, a Bible study that turned into conferences and notes that turned into a book.

It was after I became a Christian that I struggled with many relationship issues and I wrote off any chances of ever meeting a nice man. Yet in time, God led me to the man I would end up marrying. God brought him to me from the other side of the world and dropped him into my life. What are the chances? Well, 100% when it involves God. I moved to Australia (where many more miracles happened) and started a beautiful family.

Unfortunately, my struggles did not cease, even on the other side of the world. Yet here I am writing to you, fully convinced that God will not only help me, but He will also deliver me. I completely trust Him because He has never let me down. NEVER! How many people can you say that about? He will deliver me and I have full confidence, He will deliver you if you place your trust in Him. I am stronger and wiser every year and oh, so much lighter.

It is truly a gift when we can look back and see some sort of reason or sense of why we went through such hard times. It's fantastic when there is a great ending to a horrible story or situation but what about the times when we can't find any reason why we went through what we did. And even worse, what about the extended time in between, when we are in the battle. When it seems like it has gone on forever and may never end. How are we meant to fight a battle that we are drowning in?

Chapter 3
Becoming a Warrior
I can't see a way out. Where do I start?

But the Lord is with me like a mighty warrior.
Jeremiah 20:11

King Solomon made some interesting observations,

> *I have seen something else under the sun: The race is not to the swift or the battle to the strong..."* and *"No one knows what is coming- who can tell him what will happen after him? Ecclesiastes 9:11 and 10:14*

It is not our strength that wins battles. You are not a failure because you have been stuck in the same battlefield for so long. No one knows why these things happen the way they do in our lives save God alone. What I do know is that God will use them to refine you into a better person if you let him. What is the alternative? Think about that a moment. Haven't you tried everything you can think of already?

The one who created us knows exactly what we need. So how does one go about fighting a battle in realms we don't necessarily see?

Let's take a look into the life of one of my favorite warriors from history, David. He was the best at fighting battles, even better than the King of his day, Saul. When David returned from fighting a battle, the women would dance and sing,

> "Saul has slain his thousands and David his tens of thousands."
>
> 1 Samuel 18:7

This man slew tens of thousands in battle! Yet as we read about David, he had many fears and would often run and hide from confrontations. He was just an average guy with fears and failures like the rest of us, but when God took the reins of David's life, he became a mighty, valiant warrior who was victorious in battle. We have a lot to learn from him. How did he do it?

In 2 Samuel, we see how a battle is meant to be fought.

> When the Philistines heard that David had been anointed king over Israel, they went up in full force to search for him, but David heard about it and went down to the stronghold. Now the Philistines had come and spread out in the Valley of Rephaim; so David inquired of the Lord, "Shall I go and attack the Philistines? Will you deliver them into my hands?"
>
> The Lord answered him, "Go, for I will surely deliver the Philistines into your hands."
>
> So David went to Baal Perazim, and there he defeated them. He said, "As waters break out, the Lord has broken out against my enemies before me." So that place was called Baal Perazim. The Philistines abandoned their idols there, and David and his men carried them off.
>
> Once more the Philistines came up and spread out in the Valley of Rephaim; so David inquired of the Lord, and he answered, "Do not go straight up, but circle around behind them and attack them in front of the poplar trees. As soon as you hear the sound of

marching in the tops of the poplar trees, move quickly, because that will mean the Lord has gone out in front of you to strike the Philistine army." So David did as the Lord commanded him, and he struck down the Philistines all the way from Gibeon to Gezer.

2 Samuel 5:17- 25

The Philistines hated the people of God and the land of Israel. To make it worse, David had for a time associated with them and then later turned against them. To say the very least, they did not like David or Israel.

When the Philistines heard that David had been anointed the next king over Israel, they went up in full force to search for him, but David heard about it and went to a stronghold.

Find A Stronghold

As soon as David heard the enemy was coming, where did he go? He went to his stronghold. Where is your stronghold?

The Lord is a refuge for the oppressed, a stronghold in times of trouble. Psalm 9:9

In Biblical days the people would often build into the mountains or go to a high tower for their safety.

Because the power of Midian was so oppressive, the Israelites prepared shelters for themselves in mountain clefts, caves and strongholds.

Judges 6:2

Notice that the strongholds were often high up for a better vantage point. You see better when you are above it all and you gain a wider perspective. Even when strongholds were hidden in caves below, as was the case with David, the stronghold still offered a place to get away from the battle and develop a different viewpoint. God gives us that perspective when we go to Him as our stronghold. He has a clear view and can enlighten us as to what is really happening and what our best defense is.

When I am in the stronghold of my Lord, something amazing happens. Instead of fear, distress, and worry, I begin to experience the peace of God. I find myself in a different realm, a different place.

> *Your eyes will see the king in his beauty and view a land that stretches afar. In your thoughts you will ponder the former terror: "Where is that chief officer? Where is the one who took the revenue? Where is the officer in charge of the towers?"*
>
> *You will see those arrogant people no more, people whose speech is obscure, whose language is strange and incomprehensible.*
>
> *Look on Zion, the city of our festivals; your eyes will see Jerusalem, a peaceful abode, a tent that will not be moved; its stakes will never be pulled up, nor any of its ropes broken.*
>
> *There the Lord will be our Mighty One. It will be like a place of broad rivers and streams. No galley with oars will ride them, no mighty ship will sail them.*
>
> *For the Lord is our judge, the Lord is our lawgiver, the Lord is our king; it is he who will save us.*
>
> *Your rigging hangs loose: The mast is not held secure, the sail is not spread.*

> *Then an abundance of spoils will be divided and even the lame will carry off plunder. No one living in Zion will say, "I am ill"; and the sins of those who dwell there will be forgiven.* Isaiah 33:17- 24

Isaiah describes this place so well. Although he speaks about a past and future judgment of Zion, we can experience this place right now.

The person who makes God his stronghold will be fed and supplied with everything he needs. And then, my favorite part,

> *Your eyes will see the king in his beauty and view a land that stretches afar.* Isaiah 33:17

You will not only experience the presence of God, but you will begin to see the bigger picture. You will view the struggles in a different light.

> *In your thoughts you will ponder the former terror:*
> *"Where is that chief officer?*
> *Where is the one who took the revenue?*
> *Where is the officer in charge of the towers?"* Isaiah 33:18

We may word it:

> "Where is the bank officer who denied us a loan?"
> "Where is the woman who denied my application for employment?"
> "Where are those arrogant people who told me I would never amount to anything nor achieve my goals?"
> "Where is the doctor who said, 'there is no hope'?"

As you experience God in this way and ponder "the former terror", it begins to lose the grip it had on you. Your fears become stilled and a peace enters your soul. Where is the problem that was bigger than life before? Suddenly it has shrunk! You begin to relax in the knowledge that He will take care of it. It completely changes your view. You begin to see what is real and solid, what will never change, what can never be touched or moved by human nor demonic power.

> ...you will see Jerusalem, a peaceful abode (KJV version says a 'quiet home') that will not be moved; its stakes will never be pulled up, nor any of its ropes broken. There the Lord will be our Mighty One. Isaiah 33:20

It is a peaceful place that cannot be affected or altered by other humans; a place where God controls everything.

Getting to this place in times of trouble is conditional to our obedience in the way God wants us to live daily. If you look back at verse 15, it gives some clear indications of the way your life should generally look.

> Those who walk righteously and speak what is right, who reject gain from extortion and keep their hands from accepting bribes, who stop their ears against plots of murder and shut their eyes against contemplating evil. Isaiah 33:15

We should be walking righteously and speaking what is right. (I think this verse is where we get that saying, "Hear no evil, see no evil and speak no evil") Once we are in this place, Isaiah describes a new kind of lifestyle:

> There the Lord will be our Mighty One.
> It will be like a place of broad rivers and streams.
> No galley with oars will ride them,

> *No mighty ship will sail them...*
> *Your rigging hangs loose:*
> *The mast is not held secure,*
> *The sail is not spread. Isaiah 33:21-23*

I love this metaphor of a broad river where no one can steer with oars or pull the mast tight to control the direction of the boat. They just have to drift in the broad rivers and streams allowing God to control the boat.

This is the place where we stop fighting God for control. We still travel the same path but do not have the stress or burden that comes with trying to be the captain of the boat. In fact, boats controlled by anyone other than God will not be permitted in this river. When we stop fighting God and follow the path he has designed for us, we can enjoy the ride because we can trust the true captain to lead us in the way we should go.

When we are experiencing extreme grief or are recovering from another massive blow to our lives, we often come to a place where we just have to let go and trust God to sail the ship. We literally can't do anything but allow God's peace to flow over us. We have to simply let God minister to us in ways that go beyond our human understanding. Sometimes we have to put pride aside and let God and his people help us.

> *Then an abundance of spoils will be divided and even the lame will carry off plunder. No one living in Zion will say, "I am ill"; and the sins of those who dwell there will be forgiven.*
> *Isaiah 33:24*

This is a place where everyone receives abundance in equal proportions. No one is greater than the other. No one will be ill and our sins are forgiven. What a place! We will live there one day but we can let the river of God's peace live within us now simply by asking.

Ask.

Let's return to the story of David.

> *Now the Philistines had come and spread out in the Valley of Rephaim; so David inquired of the Lord, 'Shall I go and attack the Philistines? Will you deliver them into my hands?'* 2 Samuel 5:18-19

After he goes to the stronghold, David inquires of the Lord as to what to do next. He doesn't rush out to trying to tackle the problem himself.

Can you imagine what would have happened if he did? He was greatly outnumbered and humanly unprepared. He would have been slaughtered! Only when he has God's answer does he go forward to fight, knowing the outcome of the battle before he even begins!

How often do we try to go from one problem to the next, putting out fires as we go? If we would just stop for a moment before rushing into the next problem in life to ask God for some guidance, we may just find real answers to our problems. In order to hear God, we need to learn to be patient and wait.

Wait.

We need to wait on God to hear what He would have us do before we try to fix our problems. Only when we hear and obey what God leads us to do, will we find victory in our battles. As a person with limited patience, I really do understand how hard this is. But there is no other way that will conquer your problems for good.

Just Do It.

When you have heard[1] what God has told you to do, then do it!

Thank God.

When David defeated the Philistines, he gave credit to God.

> *As waters break out, the Lord has broken out against my enemies before me. 2 Samuel 5:20*

He named the place Baal Perazim, which means, "The Lord breaks out."

This is very important! When God wins a battle in your life, you need to give credit where credit is due. When people ask how you overcame your troubles, tell them the truth! God has done this to give glory through your life back to Him.

This is your witness and your testimony. It will move people because they will see the hand of God at work in your life. No one can bring peace and healing like God. No one can overcome battles like God! It will be clear to people that something special has happened in your life. If you take the credit for yourself or give that credit elsewhere, you will find a shallow and short-lived victory. Give God the glory and thank the people in your life for helping Him accomplish His purpose, His victory in your life.

I can't stress this enough! If you don't give God the glory but take the credit yourself, you have done exactly what Satan did just before his fall! The devil will tempt you to question what God has done, putting thoughts in your mind that maybe it was someone or something other than God that saved you, making you question God and His power.

---

[1] In my chapter 'Listening to God', I write more on how to hear God's voice.

David gained victory in this battle but it was not over yet. A short time later the enemy came back! The same Philistines who attacked David the first time came at him again!

So many times this is where Christians come undone. They see an amazing, powerful victory in a battle area of their life and give glory to God but then somewhere down the line, it comes back again. They wonder where God went and what happened to His victory.

Expect that you will be revisited by your enemy. I have had God come through in amazing ways in my life and yet at the next sign of trouble, I struggle with the same old fears and doubts again.

I was healed by God of an eating disorder, but there have been several times when the old feelings came back again. I had to go back to my stronghold.

I have resolved relationship issues, health issues and emotional issues, only to have them rear up again at me with the very same problems I thought I had dealt with a long time ago. I had to go back to my stronghold.

Return To Your Stronghold.

David had to go back to the stronghold and inquire of the Lord again. This is so important because when you fight a battle, the same technique that worked the first time doesn't work every time. The enemy expects the same moves. A good soldier knows that he has to adapt and change continually in wartime to outmaneuver the enemy. It would be foolish to think simply knowing how to use a gun could save you in every battle.

God is not a puzzle you can solve or a gimmick you use as a medicinal recipe. Shouting, "in Jesus' name" at the end of your demand will not resolve all of your problems. I've heard many teachings in churches that are not of God. Most of them are based on a repetitive technique that has worked for someone at some point in the past.

Like I said previously, we are individuals each in a relationship with God. Every relationship is different. Yes, we can share what worked for us but we need to make it clear that it was God who gained the victory, not the method. Other people will only find that victory if they go to the source of all victories: God Himself.

So David returns to inquire of God again. This time God tells David to fight, but look how directional God is,

> *Do not go straight up, but circle around behind them and attack them in front of the balsam trees. As soon as you hear the sound of marching in the tops of the balsam trees, move quickly, because that will mean the Lord has gone out in front of you to strike the Philistine army.*
>
> *SO DAVID DID AS THE LORD COMMANDED him and he struck down the Philistines all the way from Gibeon to Gezer.*
>
> *2 Samuel 5:23-25 (The emphasis is mine)*

David did exactly what God told him to do. He did not vary from the command, even though it was an unusual request.

When I first began to hear God in my battles, God started to ask me to do very odd things. So odd that I'm embarrassed to share them but I do so for the glory of God.

When I was young, I used to have a problem with lying. It just seemed to come naturally to me when I felt uncomfortable or needed a way out. The problem was that I lied so much that I even started to believe my lies. (I told you I had an amazing ability to create problems in my life.) It got so bad that I couldn't keep track of what I had told different people. I was addicted to lying because I was afraid of where the truth would lead me. I hated confrontation and was terrified of the consequences. Eventually, the truth finds you out. It did and my fear became reality. I hurt and even lost good friends. I tried to stop lying, but it seemed to have a hold on me.

As I grew older, I realized that this was a real problem and I needed help. This was not something I felt comfortable talking to anyone about but I wanted to change. I wanted to be free of it. I finally went to my stronghold to humbly ask God to help me and I heard God speak. He told me that when I lied (as soon as I realized I had lied), I was to go back and correct it with the truth. I told him I would do this if he made it clear to me that I was lying.

So the next day I lied about an assignment being late. I told my professor that because I had to work, I hadn't had time to do my assignment. Immediately, I had an alarm go off in my head and I felt as if I received a shock to my body. I turned to leave the room but I knew I had to immediately turn around. I went back to the professor and said, "I just lied to you, I wasn't working, I simply didn't want to do the assignment."

You can just imagine the look I got from my professor when I did that!

Another time I told someone 'I have to go to a meeting' to avoid spending time with her. I had to immediately go back and say, "I just lied to you. I'm not really going to a meeting. I am avoiding you because I am tired."

So I thought people must have thought I was going crazy. Strangely enough, when I went back to tell the truth, they already knew I was lying and were impressed I came back to tell the truth. It actually restored and renewed broken relationships!

It only took a couple of times and, amazingly, I was healed from the grip lying had on me. If the urge to lie ever arose again, I would simply remember back to the fun of telling everyone the truth and the urge would disappear.

Another time, in the midst of my eating disorder, God told me to buy a bikini. Now to someone who has an eating disorder, that's a big ask. But I did it. I thought it was a symbolic ornament and I would take it with me to remind me that one day I would have self-confidence again.

Well, one day He told me to put it on! My husband and I went to an isolated beach and I heard the voice of God clearly say, "Put on the bikini and go for a swim." I gently reminded Him that I was not at the correct weight to wear a bikini yet. He gently but firmly reminded me to simply trust and obey.

I looked around and I couldn't find a reasonable excuse not to wear it. It was an isolated beach and the only person there was my husband. So I finally succumbed and put it on. I ran across the beach and into the water. I have never entered the water so fast in my life. No one knew what kind of barrier I had just crossed except God and me. Something broke! It was a major step forward in my complete freedom from an eating bondage. One bikini led me to freedom, which led me to help hundreds of other women and men caught up in eating disorders and finally led me to write my book, 'Hungry for Life'.

God amazes me with his unusual requests. They are filled with power and grace. They certainly make the Christian life exciting and yet humbling at the same time. They are what make faith become reality.

Just recently, a friend of mine who was struggling with financial issues went to God in prayer and God spoke clearly to her telling her to give a specific amount of two hundred dollars to a specific person, a person she did not know very well. Two hundred dollars was all she had and so she prayed and prayed to make absolutely sure she understood what God was telling her.

She questioned how she would pay her bills and buy food to eat, but God's only answer was to trust Him. After more prayer, she just knew it was from God. So she gave the money to this person. She told me of the absolute joy that person experienced as an answer to her own prayer.

When my friend went home that evening she opened her power bill with a heavy heart. To her surprise, it said that she had overpaid on her last bill and it was a credit for, you guessed it, two hundred dollars exactly. An hour later, someone anonymously left a basket of food for her and her family at her front door. The next week, she landed the job she had always dreamed of, leading her to a new career.

It is through these "unusual requests" that God does a lot of work. Many times he will defeat a problem and create a blessing through a simple and unusual request. The question is do you have the guts and the humility to do what God is asking of you?

When David obeyed the unusual orders that God gave him, he found that he not only defeated his enemy, he annihilated the problem. It would never again have a hold over him. Sure, there would be murmurings here and there, rumors of uprisings, etc. but nothing that couldn't be squashed easily. When David fought, acknowledging God as his commander, God defeated his problem and built up a stronghold around and within David.

> *After the king was settled in his palace and the Lord had given him rest from all his enemies around him.*
>
> *2 Samuel 7:1*

Now that is a place I want to be, settled and at rest. It is then that we will truly experience the life that God has planned for us. The life we are meant to live.

You can read on about the exciting things God does in David's life. He does great things in God and has a lot of fun and satisfaction doing what he was meant to do. Yet we learn that we can never become complacent. Even when we are in a great place in our lives, we have to continually be spending time with God because other battles can arise. If we don't continue to go to our stronghold for answers but try to fight battles our way, then we can easily lose our way and slip down into another mess. For David, that was Bathsheba.

David should have been out fighting a battle as kings were required to do, but because of laziness, he stayed at home. He ignored God's wisdom and ended up committing adultery, getting Bathsheba pregnant and, eventually, murdering her husband to cover up his sin.

> *So if you think you are standing firm, be careful that you don't fall!* 1 Corinthians 10:12

Eventually, David repents of his sin and turns back to God. Although there were severe consequences that David had to live with, God helps David to stand up again. His story is a reminder to us that even when we fail, God can help us to stand up again.

Remember that you do not have to fight your battles alone. You can make your battles God's battles. God can help you to stand and move forward in your life. We can't see the realm in which we fight, but He can. Give Him a chance. It doesn't matter what has happened in your past or what you may have done or not done. God wants to help you.

Even if you have never prayed or talked to God, you can simply ask him to help you now. He hears your heart when it calls out to Him. God will never ask you to do something contrary to His Word, the Bible, but He will almost always take you out of your comfort zone. God loves you and wants you to overcome any battle in your life.

Chapter 4
The Warrior Within
I'm my own worst enemy.

You armed me with strength for battle.
Psalm 18:39a

How we cope with the stuff that happens to us in life directly correlates with how we are coping with the "internal" battles happening in our minds.

Internal battles include the things we deal with daily whether consciously or subconsciously. They include issues from the past, hurt or abuse, things others have said or done wrong to us (and vice versa), and our own self-image issues. They also include issues that develop over time from those hurts leading to emotions like guilt and shame.

Now the "inside" battles seem to be my personal forte, as I seem to have some sort of a gift for harboring internal problems. I have been in so many spiritual and emotional battles. I didn't ask for these battles or desire them in my life, but looking back I can see that I was the cause of most of them. I bring this stuff on myself! That's what gets me. I do such a good job that Satan and his demonic realm can go have a coffee and kick back for a while.

Now, believe me, I would rather blame it on someone else. But as time passed on, I started to see a repeated pattern where the only common denominator was me. I was forced to come to grips with the ugly truth – I do a great job at stuffing up my life without anyone else's help. I once read a great truth somewhere that said that once you realize you are the cause of your problems, then you know where to begin to solve your problems.

When I first became a Christian I was in the midst of an eating disorder that consumed my whole life. I wasn't battling anyone else. The battle was going on inside of me and it nearly took my life.

How do you fight battles that no one else knows about? I was embarrassed and hid that battle for 7 years. Even my own mother knew nothing about it! I tried to fight it with my whole being. Every day I would start with a "fresh slate" in my mind and every day I would fail. Over and over again I would repeat this pattern day after day.

I knew I needed to trust God for my healing but every time I tried to be free of this problem, I would fall in a heap again. I just felt so out of control.

Paul wrote about a similar struggle going on within him. Although this verse seems a bit confusing to many, I love this verse because it perfectly displays what my brain looked like when I was in the midst of such inner turmoil.

> *I do not understand what I do. For what I want to do I do not do, but what I hate I do... I know that nothing good lives in me, that is, in my sinful nature. For I have the desire to do what is good, but I cannot carry it out. For what I do is not the good I want to do; no, the evil I do not want to do- this I keep on doing. Now if I do what I do not want to do, it is no longer I who do it, but it is sin living in me that does it.*
>
> *So I find this law at work: When I want to do good, evil is right there with me. For in my inner being I delight in God's law; but I see another law at work in the members of my body, waging war against the law of my mind and making me a prisoner of the law of sin at work within my members. What a wretched man I am! Who will rescue me from this body of death? Romans 7:15-24*

Other internal battles I struggled with included overcoming fears, depression, guilt, shame, addictions, low self-worth and failure. The problem with these battles is that you can't share them with other people either due to the sensitivity of the problems or the reputation that you would like to keep up – mainly that you are a somewhat sane and nice person. This is magnified if you are in any sort of leadership position where people are looking up to you.

The other reason I didn't share many of my internal battles with other people is that I didn't want to hear their advice. I had already tried every possible human solution. I didn't want to hear another person say, "Just stop eating so much" in answer to an eating disorder. Or to hear some advice that is contrary to what I believe like, "Just lie about it, no one will ever know". I knew I needed help that went beyond human thinking to someone who could actually solve my problems.

When God brings me victoriously through a battle, I find that He first confronts the real issues and then, trains me to defeat the enemy (which could include myself, others, and/or spiritual forces). It is all due to Him that I win, as I don't have the strength to fight battles on my own. I tried many times to do it my way, but my way doesn't gain the victory. I may gain little steps on my own, but I inevitably slide back into the mess I was in when I first started. It is only with God's help that I can gain the momentum I need to win the battle and never return to that battlefield again. When I place God in charge of my life, my battles suddenly become His battles. God changes my perspective about the battle in front of me and with God on my side, things don't look as daunting as they did before.

It's like what the Lord said to King Jehoshaphat,

> *Do not be afraid or discouraged because of this vast army. For the battle is not yours, but God's.* 2 Chronicles 20:15

Revelation 19:11 describes Christ as the Commander of the Armies of Heaven. He is the only one truly qualified to fight the kind of battles I'm talking about. He does it with a simple command. It is so simple that He humbles mankind every time He does it.

So how does He do it? How does He train us, the weak and weary, to fight and win battles in a glorious way? He starts like any other Army General. He takes his warriors through basic training and works them up to the Special Forces. To fight battles successfully we need to train.

Basic training is very much like the basic training you would find for any army. It's hard work and very humbling. It is also very personalized, uniquely designed for each individual that He created. I can give you examples of things I've been through so that you get an idea of what this training looks like, but please understand that you will have completely different experiences to me. You also need to be aware that you don't go through basic training with God just once. You will go through it again and again, before every battle you are about to fight.

No soldier learns to fight in the middle of a battle. To send an untrained soldier onto the battlefield would be a death sentence. Soldiers have to be trained, learn the skills, practice the skills and have experience under their belt before heading out to a battlefield. Only then is a soldier ready for the unknown.

You may already have a battle going on full bore in your life. Let me say that God will not train you in the midst of that battle. Your training will come in the most unexpected places because God needs to train you where you can learn and not be distracted.

In the midst of my eating disorder, I had a full-blown battle going on within me. I couldn't hear anything God may have been saying to me because all I could hear was my failure. Although I would hear God in other areas of my life, when it came to my battle with food, all I could hear was silence in the heavens.

In the midst of depression, you're not able to hear about the joy that God has in store. While struggling with finances, seeing God's abundance becomes impossible. While dealing with the loss of someone close or a marriage breakdown, a person is already worn down, exhausted and consumed with his or her own thoughts and cannot conceive how God could help.

When I am consumed with a battle in my life, unfortunately, I am locked into one kind of thinking- the impossible, failure, doomed kind of thinking. I am set in my ways and not very moldable or teachable in my spirit. Yet if I am distracted from my problem, God has a chance to move in and train me so I can go back to my problem as a stronger person.

When I was struggling with serious battles in my life, I noticed that God would teach me things in other areas of my life, things that later would transfer over to help me in my "battle" areas.

For example, when I was battling with an eating disorder, I struggled with control issues. I could trust God to be in control of every area of my life except my eating. God wanted me to hand the reins over to him and allow Him to guide me through to freedom, but I just didn't know how. I tried to let go and trust Him but I just couldn't. I didn't have the skill and I couldn't learn the skill while I was in the midst of the problem. I would hear God telling me to trust Him and I would. I would trust God until I blew it and then I'd take back the control and try to fix what I had done wrong. God knew I needed to learn not only to listen to Him but to obey what He asked me to do to get through this battle and into complete freedom.

I began to hear God calling me to learn obedience. It would start with simple commands, so simple that honestly, I am embarrassed to write about them. I hesitate to share this example with you because anyone who has never experienced God in this way could find it hard to understand. Yet I share because I want to show that God works in such unexpected ways.

One day while walking home, I was in the middle of a parking lot and I noticed a piece of paper blow by, a bit of trash, and I just kept walking. I was quite far away from the paper when I heard God say, "Go back and pick up that piece of paper."

At first, I thought maybe I was experiencing mild insanity. I took a few more steps and there it was again, "Go back and pick it up."

By now my heart was beating faster and I started to feel silly. I began to wrestle with the command in my mind. "This is stupid. Why would I walk all the way back there to pick up a piece of rubbish that has probably already blown away?"

Yet the urge just got stronger and stronger and it wouldn't leave me alone. Finally, I gave in. I walked back, ignored a couple of awkward looks from some people in the parking lot and picked up that piece of paper.

Now after all this, you may be thinking what I was thinking at the time, that there would be something of significance written on that piece of paper. Nope, not a thing. Now I felt even more silly than I did when the thought first entered my brain. I put it in the trash and began my journey home again. I felt humiliated and was confused as to why I had had to do this little exercise.

As I walked, I felt God's presence with me. He knew my hurt and humiliation over what He had asked me to do. I expressed to him, quietly in my mind, that I thought He would ask me to do great things not silly, embarrassing things like chasing a piece of paper, a piece of trash. Yet He gently brought forth the question that if I couldn't do something as simple as picking up a piece of paper, how could I do something complex? I needed to learn to obey orders without understanding the purpose behind them. I simply had to trust my Commander and know that He has had much more experience in fighting battles than me.

I wish I had simply accepted that and walked on...

but a little bit of anger surfaced over what I felt was a silly exercise. I mean it was just a waste of time and effort, a trivial exercise. I let that anger rise up in my heart against God which led to a very self-righteous opinion about what had just happened.

Suddenly I experienced the power of God in his rebuke and at the same time, I felt the humility of Christ. Although it is hard to put this into human words, the experience of God's teaching may have sounded a bit like this (in a very loud voice):

"Do you think that I have never experienced humiliation? I the Creator of the world and all that is held within it? I lowered myself to become one of my creation, endured ridicule, was stripped naked and beaten until I was unrecognizable. I went through the unimaginable as I walked the road that led to my death.

You have no idea what was said and done to me. People spat in my face and turned their faces away from what stood before them. I did nothing but heal my people and confront the evil in their lives. Yet I was hung naked on a piece of wood in front of humanity who laughed and mocked. I died and defeated death for my creation so that they may have new life. And yet I still give them a choice and watch them stupidly walk away and destroy themselves. I think I know a little about humiliation, don't you?"

Completely silenced, I no longer questioned that exercise. I decided it might be wise not to question God again when He asked me to do something.

Of course, if you know me and my ongoing quest to understand the reason why I should do something before I do it, you would know that God had to teach me this lesson again (sadly, many times).

Another time I was watching the television and was into my show when again I heard His voice that lives in my conscience urging me to turn the television off and go to bed.

Now I love stories and I feel compelled to know the ending of any story that I start to watch. I didn't want to turn off the television. Again the thoughts began to fly in my head. "Surely, I'm not hearing right. Why should I?"

Yet the urge just wouldn't leave me. I knew I was not being obedient and suddenly a commercial came on for a horror show later that night. I saw it and it was shocking. It made me sick. I turned off the television and went to bed.

I had a nightmare that night which was so awful and real that I wished I had never seen those images. Again I was reminded that my obedience was for my own good. God doesn't simply throw orders out; He has a reason for everything, even when we don't see it.

Sometimes God trained me by asking me to do nothing! When I was looking for my first teaching job, I remember clearly hearing God say, "Just wait and the job will come to you."

I was okay with that for about a week, then impatience got the better of me. I spent hours making a detailed resume and spent nearly a week making copies and sending them with cover letters to about thirty schools. I waited and waited. I didn't hear back from a single one of those schools, ever.

After letting me marinate in the aftermath of exhaustion, disappointment and failure, God came through on His word. Two schools which I hadn't even applied to, who had heard from family and friends that I needed a job, offered me a position. He not only blessed me with a job but doubly blessed me that I had to choose which job I wanted. I began to understand the skill of waiting.

There were several other little incidences that God used to further test and refine me. When I didn't obey, there were always a couple of not-so-nice consequences. Let me just say here that the consequences of disobedience to God are never nice; they're annoying and humiliating. I know this because I tend to be a slow learner.

As time passed, my brain started to compute that I would rather be obedient and look stupid, than to suffer the consequences of disobedience. I was now ready to listen and I was determined to obey anything I heard Him say, no matter how silly or stupid it was.

So I started to do what I felt God was leading me to do, no matter where I was or who I was with. After a couple more "simple" instructions, suddenly I moved on to the amazing. I started to see a glimpse of the purpose behind God's requests.

For example, I was sitting at a table eating lunch when I heard His voice urging me to ask the woman beside me about her baby and to tell her God loves her. I looked at the lady next to me, who did not have a baby or look pregnant. "She is going to think I am mad", came the thoughts, "I don't even know this lady."

But I decided to obey.

With my heart beating madly, I quietly and nervously asked her about her baby. She looked at me as if she had seen a ghost and asked, "How did you know?" I simply said, "I felt God leading me to ask you and to tell you that He loves you."

Through her tears, she explained to me that only days ago she had lost her baby in a miscarriage and hadn't told anyone. She felt that God had not cared and had been praying for some sort of sign. She was reassured and so was I that God did truly care.

As I began to learn the art of hearing God and obeying His voice, I found the skills I had learned transferred into the battlefield of my eating disorder. I was suddenly able to hear God speak. What seemed like years of silence was broken and I began to understand that the battle was so full-on and loud, that it had blocked my sense of hearing. God had to take me out of the battle to train my ears to hear and my heart to obey so that I could go back into the battle and follow His guidance to freedom. It became lasting freedom and complete freedom which I still experience today.

When God goes before you into your battles, He never loses.

> *Who is this King of glory? The Lord strong and mighty, the Lord mighty in battle. Psalm 24:8*

Chapter 5

The State of the Heart
This God Stuff Doesn't Seem To Work For Me.

> *The Lord does not look at the things man looks at. Man looks at the outward appearance, but the Lord looks at the heart.*
> 1 Samuel 16:7b

Many Christians and good people wonder why they do not feel close to God and hear Him speak into their lives, especially during times of suffering or hardship. They may go to church each week and may even read their Bible daily, yet don't feel that the relationship has ever moved past an acquaintance level.

The state of your heart is an extremely important factor in your relationship with God. If your heart is not right, it will block wisdom and understanding from the Lord.

> *They are darkened in their understanding and separated from the life of God because of the ignorance that is in them due to the hardening of their hearts. Ephesians 4:18*

There are two conditions of the heart: one is set like a rock, the other is moldable, like playdough.

The heart that is set like rock is characterized by the following attributes: hardened, bitter, resentful, slanderous, blaming, judgmental and the continuous feeling of having been judged, offended, fearful, dark, distracted, prideful, enslaved, sick and, finally, death. When your heart is in this state, you endure suffering along with torment.

The heart that is moldable like play dough is characterized by the following attributes: soft, teachable, moveable, compassionate, giving, sacrificial, confident, humble, loved, loving, focused, free, light, trusting, approachable, gifted, strong, healthy, saved and, finally, full of life. When your heart is in this state, you endure suffering with hope. You understand that if entrusted to God, suffering can refine you.

Picture a mold of something. Let's say, for example, a mold of a hand. If you were to put playdough in the mold, you could quite easily push it around until it was in the mold just right and then if you removed the mold, it would look very much like a hand; how the mold was cast.

Now try to imagine putting a rock into that mold. It could be done but it would take a lot of effort. You would have to get a chisel and a grinding saw to shape it. You would have to keep putting it in and out of the mold and breaking more pieces off to fit it just right.

Now imagine the state of your heart. Is it a pliable heart that can be moved through God's teaching? Is it humble, open to learning, quick to recognize a wrong and easily moved to make things right? Or is your heart set in its ways, not wanting to hear about the stuff in your life that is holding you back?

Can you admit you make mistakes and have weaknesses? Can you comprehend that you may be in the wrong and have to do something about it? Or do you feel you have every right to be the way you are and who does God think He is to go about changing things anyway?

Let me ask you some questions and I want you to really have a hard look at yourself and answer them truthfully:

How do you respond to someone when you are told that, "you are wrong"?

    a. Do you get angry and begin to verbally attack the other person?
    b. Do you call them some sort of inferior name and walk away?
    c. Do you sincerely have a look at yourself and weigh up what was said- maybe even make some adjustments to your life and let go of anything that does not apply?
    d. Do you agree without question and generally feel worthless as a person?

What do you do when you find out that you have made a mistake?

    a. Do you apologize and set out to make it right?
    b. Deny it ever happened.
    c. Justify that you were not to blame.
    d. Blame it on someone else.
    e. Say nothing yet continue to feel like a failure.

(If you answered "a", when exactly was the last time you specifically said, "I am sorry, will you forgive me?" to someone you offended?)

How do you respond when you are shown some ugly personality traits about yourself that someone would like you to work on?

    a. Do you get angry?
    b. Do you bring out even uglier traits to show the former were nothing in comparison?
    c. Do you examine your ways and try to change?
    d. Do you simply agree and feel hopeless to change?

How do you feel when you politely ask someone to move and they tell you to "---- off"? What are your thoughts about that person?

    a. "Man, they're having a hard day."
    b. "?!@#?" (Responding with even more graphic

      language)
- c. "I'm glad I don't look like that piece of trash."
- d. "Wow, that person needs some help."
- e. Continue to marinate in the feeling of "what on earth did I do to cause that?"

I was a teacher for 11 years in various classroom settings but I mostly taught high-school-aged students. I love teens!! They question everything and for the most part, they really do want to find out answers to life, no matter what it is that they find out.

However, there are a few that do not want to be in class (surprise, surprise) and make that very clear from the moment they first enter the room. Their body language is closed off and they won't even look at you. They sit slumped in their chair and roll their eyes when you address them. When you begin to teach, they are the ones that mutter under their breath (but just loud enough for everyone to hear) comments like: "yeah, duh, we already know that" or "what a waste of time" or "who cares?"

Now my goal as a teacher is to train my students to do their best so that when they leave school they will be prepared for the challenges that are awaiting them. I want to help them to achieve their dreams and goals. But if a student won't even give me the chance to teach, they will not likely receive the help they need.

What they don't understand is that they are only hurting themselves. I don't have to put up with it, I could send them out of the class and many teachers do. I try to look past it and keep persevering. But I keep focusing on readjusting their heart- their stinky attitude. We've all met people like this and have ourselves at times been like this.

What is the one thing that will stop you from ever knowing God, stop answers to your biggest questions and interfere with the most amazing life God has lined up for you? Your own stinkin' pride. It's the biggest barrier you'll ever face. The thing that stops spiritual maturity, well any maturity, is the refusal to change because you believe you are right.

Again it is the state of your heart that determines how quickly you will mature. The more pride, the harder the heart. If you feel that people often offend you or that you don't seem to have any close friendships at all, it's worth taking some time to ask God to help you with your heart attitude.

God, as the master artist, has a mold for our hearts. He adjusts our hearts to fit that mold. If our heart material is soft and pliable, it is much easier to work with and will fit the mold quicker. But if our heart material is like concrete, due to pride, God will still work to get it in the mold but He will have to chisel and break pieces off to form it to the mold. This way is more difficult and causes more pain but God will still continue to work to get our heart to fit the mold.

God does have a mold and it is His son Jesus Christ. He is changing us every day to be more and more like Jesus and He won't stop until we look just like the original cast. We are to be like Jesus, the example set by God for our world to follow.

How do we soften our heart attitude? Ask God for His help. When you make mistakes, apologize and be open to change.

I find the following passage from the Bible is a great way to see where I am in my attitude by substituting my own name for the word "Love" or "it":

> *Love is patient, love is kind. It does not envy, it does not boast, it is not proud. It does not dishonor others, it is not self-seeking, it is not easily angered, it keeps no record of wrongs.*
>
> *Love does not delight in evil but rejoices with the truth. It always protects, always trusts, always hopes, always perseveres-1 Corinthians 13:4-7*

So I question myself: Am I patient? Am I kind? Am I envious? Am I boastful? And so on. If I am not acting in love then I am off the track that God has set before me and I need to ask Him to help me.

Your heart needs to either become pliable or you will be chiseled. I have experienced both and I have chosen to make myself pliable because the other way just hurts.

So how do we keep our hearts more like playdough than like a rock?

Well, that is the reason Jesus came to us. He is the only one that can move the heart from the first condition to the latter. He begins his work as soon as you invite Him to take control of your heart. You do this by confessing and declaring that Jesus really is God and believing in your heart this is true.

> ..."The word is near you; it is in your mouth and in your heart," that is, the word of faith message concerning faith that we proclaim: If you declare with your mouth, "Jesus is Lord,"' and believe in your heart that God raised him from the dead, you will be saved. For it is with your heart that you believe and are justified, and it is with your mouth that you profess your faith and are saved. Romans 10:10

You may have heard people say, "You need to ask Jesus into your heart". As a child, I used to imagine a mini Jesus setting up home inside my physical heart. I just couldn't understand how He could fit in there. Later, due to this misunderstanding, I would doubt His presence. It just didn't make sense. How could Jesus reside in my heart? Was I possessed? I didn't feel any different. I still made mistakes, so did that mean He wasn't there? Did I do something wrong?

When Solomon completed the task to build a temple for the name of the Lord, he realized the vast greatness of the Lord could not be contained within such a small structure. Upon completion, he asked God, *"But will God really dwell on earth with men? The heavens, even the highest heavens, cannot contain you. How much less this temple I have built!"* 1 Kings 8:27

God is everywhere at all times, yet He gives us this picture of being within the heart so we understand our heart is His focus, the base from which He will work in our lives.

The heart is the first place you will begin to experience Jesus. You will feel Him in there doing some serious construction projects as He shapes how you view situations and deal with the experiences of life. Slowly you will begin to notice that you are changing into a better person, completely dependent on Christ but not upon anyone else. Adopted into a safe place and completely provided for, you begin to experience complete freedom from the world you are living in. More things will begin to make sense and your load will become lighter. You will become focused and clear, working out of a truth that transcends our world and its thinking. All these things will stem from your heart and you won't be able to explain it with your brain.

Yet it is only upon invitation that Christ will begin His work within your heart. He can transform your heart from its set ways into freedom, yet you have to ask Him to do it. This is what keeps humanity humble. Remember that it was arrogance and pride that led to the fall of many kings and even the angel of light to become an angel of death.

> *You said in your HEART, "I will ascend to heaven; I will raise my throne above the stars of God"...*
> *In the pride of your HEART, you say, "I am a god; I sit on the throne of a god..."*

> *Your HEART became proud on account of your beauty, and you corrupted your wisdom because of your splendor.*
> *Extracted from Isaiah 14:13, Ezekiel 28:1-19 (Emphasis mine)*

When you ask God to come into your life and make your heart more like His, you can expect (you may have guessed it by now) suffering. Yes, there it is again. Suffering and going through difficult journeys in our lives help make our hearts pliable. Expect suffering to come.

> *For it has been granted to you on behalf of Christ not only to believe in him, but also to suffer for him. Philippians 1:29*

It amazes me that, even today, when I experience suffering, I am taken by surprise every time! I know that I am not alone. Too often people think that, if and when they become Christians, they will not experience suffering anymore.

That simply is not true. Even as Christians when we go through times of hardships, it is easy to think that Jesus has abandoned us or that we have done something wrong. We waste too much time wondering what we have done to upset God and questioning the very character of God. We question God and wonder if He has somehow deserted us in our time of suffering.
Thoughts play over and over in our minds, "Surely if I were closer to God, then I would not be going through this."

We want to think that God would not allow us to experience suffering.

That is not what the Bible, the very word of God, teaches. Sadly, many churches and Christians fail to prepare those who want to follow Christ for what follows. Yes, suffering will come. It is guaranteed. I would challenge you to find one person in the Bible who did not suffer. Even Jesus suffered. If we are followers of Jesus, why would we not encounter suffering?

> *Dear friends, do not be surprised at the painful trial you are suffering, as though something strange were happening to you.*
> 1 Peter 4:12

> *But join with me in suffering for the gospel, by the power of God.*
> 2 Timothy 1:8

> *Now if we are children, then we are heirs- heirs of God and co-heirs with Christ, if indeed we share in his sufferings in order that we may also share in his glory. I consider that our present sufferings are not worth comparing with the glory that will be revealed in us. Romans 8:17-18*

Everyone will experience suffering of some sort in this world, Christian or non-Christian. Giving your life into the hands of God will not prevent suffering. It will not get rid of trials and temptations. Expect suffering in your life. It is there for a purpose.

> *For the creation was subjected to frustration, not by its own choice, but by the will of the one who subjected it, in hope that the creation itself will be liberated from its bondage to decay and brought into the glorious freedom of the children of God.*
> Romans 8:20-21

Jesus did not come into the world to get rid of suffering. He came here to overcome it and defeat it. He teaches His followers to do the same. That is why Peter can say,
> *But rejoice that you participate in the sufferings of Christ, so that you may be overjoyed when his glory is revealed. 1 Peter 4:13*

If we did not suffer, we would not experience the power of God in our lives. Suffering strengthens our spiritual heart muscles. When we begin to trust God in our present situation, no matter what we are going through, we will begin to know God. We become intimate with God as we travel through personal suffering. This builds our faith. As Jesus works in miraculous ways to bring us through that suffering, He makes us more like Him. He shows us more of who He is. We begin to understand His thoughts and purposes for our lives.

What is the heart? Physically, the heart is where we draw our energy. It is the home base that everything else depends on to function properly. It is the life source. If stopped beating, life would end. In the spiritual realm, the heart is also the place where we draw our thoughts, dreams and purpose. It is the base from which morality is set and choices are made. It is the throne room where we have to decide who is the King, the Leader, and the Boss of our lives. Whatever or whoever is on that throne will dictate our choices and direction in life.

Some people have a concept on the throne-like popularity, riches or success. They will revolve their lives around this concept. The concept becomes more important than people, including the person upon whose heart it rules. They are like gems that are pretty to look at, but in reality they are cold and unmoving. Our concept of a successful life determines the image we try to portray to others.

Image is drawn from imagination. It's a mirage. It is based on comparison. We constantly strive to achieve a projected image but as soon as we draw near, it seems to change or move every time. Look at the people who seemingly have everything and are "successful" by the world's standards. Do they seem happy, fulfilled and content with life? Most of our rehabilitation facilities, psychiatric centers and cemeteries are filled with concept-driven people.

> *But if you harbor bitter envy and selfish ambition in your hearts, do not boast about it or deny the truth. Such 'wisdom' does not come down from heaven but is earthly, unspiritual, of the*

> *devil. For where you have envy and selfish ambition, there you find disorder and every evil practice. James 3:14-15*

Those who wish to put themselves on the throne and run their own lives are in real trouble when things go wrong. Where can they go for help? Who can they turn to for answers? Their wisdom is only based on what they know and understand which is very limited. There always seems to be something missing in life. They spend a lot of time distracting themselves from this question by keeping busy and continually trying new things because if they stop too long and think about life, it becomes overwhelming. In the end, they only have themselves to blame and spend a lot of time wondering, "what if?"

Those who invite Jesus to be on the throne in their life, take a huge leap when it comes to trust, but as struggles come, they find that Jesus meets their needs and goes beyond their expectations.

Jesus created the command center of your heart. He knows exactly what you need to keep this vital muscle strengthened and working. He knows what we need to live a fulfilling, vibrant life instead of chasing a mirage.

Chapter 6
Covenant or Contract
Christianity is just a bunch of rules, isn't it?

> *I will establish my covenant as an everlasting covenant between me and you and your descendants after you for the generations to come, to be your God.*
> Genesis 17:7

God loves covenant, not contracts. Although in today's world they are often seen as one and the same, there is a significant difference. While both represent a commitment between two people, they differ in the way people approach and use these commitments. So what's the difference?

A **Contract** is legally binding and is used to hold the other party accountable. It is a signed agreement between both parties to exchange one good for another.

A **Covenant** is a spiritual agreement, a pledge made by one who loves the other and wants to display commitment.

A **Contract** finishes when the job is done.

A **Covenant** is for life.

A **Contract** is focused on the outcomes, not the person.

In a **Covenant**, a person's worth is more important than what they have done or acquired.

A **Contract** can feel overshadowing or threatening.

A **Covenant** encourages the other person to feel safe.

If a person in the **Contract** gets a better offer, he will look for a loophole in the contract to get out of it.

A person in a **Covenant** will steer clear of a better offer, so it will not be tempting to hurt their covenant partner.

If one doesn't follow through on a **Contract**, then the other will take the matter to a higher authority so that the offender will be punished by law.

If someone breaks a **Covenant**, the other is concerned about the person and will support that person to make it right again.

A **Contract** can be broken.

A **Covenant** is giving oneself to another as a perpetual pledge.

Covenants can be included in contracts.

It is so important to understand this because it is foundational to the Christian faith and will affect the way we perceive God.

God is a God of covenants not contracts.

Many people think God relates to them contractually; that He is always watching out for those who break His commands so He can be quick to punish. God is pictured as a lawyer, jury and judge, and the evidence is stacked against humanity.

Trying to please God, people focus in on His laws to see what they need to "do" to be "successful" in God's eyes. Then there is the additional pressure of humans continually adding onto God's law to make even more laws. Add to that all the unstated, unwritten laws that we just expect of each other and in the end, "Law" can easily take over. Humanity just cannot keep up with all the laws and "fail" to keep so many commands. Interestingly enough, when you continually fail at something, you eventually give up trying at all!

God's law is perfect and no one is able to keep His law perfectly. So humanity is left feeling rejected and hopeless. People may think to themselves, "What's the point of trying to know God? I'm already condemned. I'll never be good enough." In this scenario, there is no hope. This is the substance of contracts. Contracts focus on expectations and don't leave room for failure.

The law was introduced in the Old Testament and God does take His law very seriously. We need the law to set boundaries for living. If there was no law, society could not operate. It is the law that sets a line for human conscience to follow. Law was made for our relationships. If we didn't have the law, we would continually hurt others and ourselves.

Imagine children playing without any rules. They could run in the streets without any concern for traffic. They could start fires or drink chemicals. If they were angry, they could throw a rock at someone's window. Or if they didn't like someone, they could just hit them. You get the idea. We are born with a selfish will and a desire to get our own way. If the law did not exist, we could not exist in relationships with each other.

God did create the Law but He knew we couldn't fulfill a contractual agreement to keep the law and gain eternal salvation. So God made a Covenant to us through His Son, Jesus Christ.

A wonderful thing happened when Jesus came along. Love entered the world and people were forgiven for not being perfect. They were even forgiven for breaking the law! Did this eliminate the need for the law? Jesus said,

> *"Do not think that I have come to abolish the Law or the Prophets; I have not come to abolish them but to fulfill them."*
> Matthew 5:17

Jesus wanted His creation to understand that the law was created for relationship. He wanted to shift humankind's attention from being so caught up about the details of the law, to putting relationships first. Yes, the law is important, but people are more important.

He summed up all the laws into two commandments:

> *Jesus replied: "Love the Lord your God with all your heart and with all your soul and with all your mind. This is the first and greatest commandment. And the second is like it: 'Love your neighbor as yourself.' All the Law and the Prophets hang on these two commandments." Matthew 22:37-40*

It is through a relationship with Jesus Christ that we can bypass the contractual law through His Covenant pledge to us. God is Holy and expects His law to be fulfilled. He knew as humans we were not divine and could not accomplish this on our own. He sent a mirror image of Himself into the world to fulfill the law on our behalf. All we need to do is set aside our pride, ask forgiveness for not fulfilling the law, thank Jesus for what He has done and commit to a relationship with Him.

it is through relationships with others that we are able to show God's love and learn how to encourage and help others. We don't encourage anyone by demanding they follow our interpretation of the law or our expectations. We encourage others the same way God encourages us, through relationship and showing love. Let your example be motivation for those around you to change.
Satan has focused humanity on contractual terms and failure. He reminds people of their mistakes and sins, telling them that they

are unforgivable. He tries to convince us we will never be good enough. Don't even try coming to God because He will reject you. What a lie that so many have believed!

God will continually fulfill His covenant to you in that He will always pursue you with His love and support you to make that covenant right again. We can choose to say, "No" and walk away from that covenant and God, but He will always be there waiting and willing to support you, should you ever change your mind.

When I had children, I caught a glimpse of what it must have been like to bring forth humanity into this world. As I held each child for the first time, I had an inexplicable depth of love for them that has never left me.

As I raised my children, I began to understand the deep desire within God's heart. There is nothing I want more than to have a relationship with my children. I want the very best for them and I hope that they trust me and can confide in me. I will protect and defend them, yet also discipline and correct them. Although they may not agree with me or even like me some days, I am doing what I do because I think it is best for them. I do all of this because I love them. I love my relationship with them.

I don't want to just coexist with my children; I want a great relationship with them that lasts. Yet how do they know I love them? They simply have to experience it for themselves, and, as time passes, they can begin to see that even when I had to be stern at times, I acted out of love. As we spend time together, they learn more about me. As our relationships develop, they trust me and see that through time and trials, I am committed to them and I am on their side!

We begin all relationships with faith that they will work because that's the way relationships are designed to be. A relationship with God is no different.

If you are the type of person who wants proof before you believe in God, I'm sad to tell you that God won't be pressured by His creation to do anything. He's the boss, not you. He is God after all. He doesn't have to perform to your demands. The Creator is not subject to His creation.

According to Matthew 7:6, Proverbs 9:8 and 23:9, it would be useless for God to attempt to "prove" everything to you if your heart is not open to see or understand.

In the movie *Indiana Jones and the Last Crusade*, there is a scene that, in my opinion, shows so clearly what faith in God is like.

Indiana is following instructions from his Father's old, leather-bound diary, listing the steps he will need to follow to lead him to the Holy Grail. He gets to the final step called the "leap of faith." Indiana finds himself standing on the edge of a cliff and looking at a wide chasm with the ground so far below, it is out of sight. This chasm stands between him and the cave that holds the Holy Grail which will bring life back to his dying father.

Indiana knows that a "leap of faith" means stepping out into mid-air and having faith that somehow all will be okay and he will manage to make it to the other side. But knowing this does not relieve his fear of it. It might as well be the Grand Canyon because no human could clear this chasm with a leap. If he falls, he will plummet hundreds of meters to his death. He's sweating and scared as he realizes he is about to die, but he has to do this. He sticks his foot out, holds his breath and leans forward to take a step.

Suddenly, his foot strikes an invisible bridge. As he walks, the bridge becomes apparent. It's been there all along but he didn't see it until he stepped out in faith. Once he took the step, it seemed so obvious. How could anyone miss it? When he reaches the other side, he scoops up some gravel and throws it over the path he just crossed, so others could see what seemingly isn't there.

I find it is very similar with God. He is there, although you may not see Him. What is so obvious and real to me is invisible to others because they have not taken a step, no, a leap of faith.

I was a person who didn't particularly love change and I had a real fear of the unknown, so taking what seemed at the time like a blind leap, took an amazing amount of faith. I wanted to test it first, by taking a little step because a step allows you to keep one foot in the control of your world. But to follow God requires a leap of faith. A leap is when you throw yourself in, no holds barred.

Once you decide in your heart that you are committed to following Him, no matter what the cost, and take that leap to blindly follow what you don't completely understand, you will find your foot on solid ground. What was invisible will become very visible and you'll wonder how you could have ever doubted before.

Just so you are aware, this is not a seasonal commitment. You can't fool God by believing in your mind that, "I'll follow you for a while and see what happens". This requires the mindset of, "I will follow you for the rest of my life, no matter if I ever see you or hear you. I am committed to you God, no matter if I look like a fool to everyone else. I will stick by this commitment no matter what troubles may come. I can't do this life without you, so I'd rather have relationship with you than live an empty life". It is an all in kind of commitment. There is no going back!

Being a Christian is quite easy, all you have to do is proclaim Jesus to be the Lord of your life, to believe it in your heart and profess it with your mouth. Yet the weight, the cost, of that statement that "Jesus is Lord of my life", means that you will lose your life so that you may find it. You will have to kiss your old life, the one that you were in charge of, goodbye.

For me, that didn't seem a big ask. My life was going in circles before I found Jesus. Yes, there were occasional good times and on a surface level all looked okay, but deep within I was dissatisfied and couldn't find contentment or peace within my soul. I couldn't keep up with the world's agenda, as I was never good enough, smart enough or wealthy enough. No one appreciated me for who I really was underneath. I was always putting on masks and playing a part for other people. I was always concerned about what others thought, said or did. I didn't think freedom, peace or real joy were experiences to be grasped until I experienced them for myself.

C.S. Lewis describes this leap of faith in such a beautiful way in his book *Mere Christianity*:

"Good things as well as bad, you know,
are caught by a kind of infection.

If you want to get warm you must stand near the fire:
if you want to be wet you must get into the water.

If you want joy, power, peace, eternal life,
you must get close to, or even into, the thing that has them.

They are not a sort of prize
which God could, if He chose, just hand out to anyone.
They are a great fountain of energy and beauty
spurting up at the very centre of reality.

If you are close to it, the spray will wet you:
if you are not, you will remain dry.

Once a man is united to God, how could he not live forever?"[2]

Why stand on the side of the fountain, only to feel the "mist" of the goodness of God when you can jump into the water and experience them firsthand. Yes, you will lose your old self but did I mention that you would gain a new life? Yes, you will not be the

---

[2] Mere Christianity-1952; Harper Collins: 2001; 176-177

boss of it, but the one who created you will now lead you in a life beyond your wildest imagination if you will just have faith.

Why does faith seem so distant and impossible to have?

Faith seems hard to find or possess because we have lost the ability to trust. We live in an age of contracts, where you have to fill out insurance forms before you begin any activity under the sun and sign agreements that you will not hold anyone responsible if something goes wrong. It is not uncommon to file pre-nuptial contracts before entering into a marriage. There are lawsuits if any mistakes are made and divorce when relationships get too hard. Competitiveness and cattiness are stylish. People who seem like friends quickly use and abuse relationships so they can get ahead.

We're used to people not showing up in organizations due to their "busyness" and people changing jobs like they change their clothes. We don't know what trust and commitment are anymore. We find it hard to comprehend a God who will always love us (no matter what we do), always be there for us, always protect us and provide for us.

Even as new Christians, many can be quick to lose faith when things don't go as they imagined it would. Ugly thoughts form in the back of our mind, shouting out to God, "See, I knew you would let me down!" or "You don't really love me."

It's as if we wait for proof of something that has gone wrong so that we can pin on God- when really (if we are honest) we are just pouting that God is not performing to our demands. But if we are always testing God, we haven't jumped into the ocean of faith. We need to remember that trust in God is a journey that He will lead. Don't worry if you doubt and waiver, just keep asking God to help you and guide you.

Even in the Bible, God's people of faith had their moments of doubt too.

Look at Peter. In the excitement of seeing Jesus walk on water, he had the courage to literally step out in faith; yet even though he knew Jesus and talked with Him daily, he still had his times of doubt.

> *During the fourth watch of the night, Jesus went out to them, walking on the lake. When the disciples saw him walking on the lake, they were terrified. "It's a ghost," they said and cried out in fear.*

Imagine what you would think, if you saw someone walking towards you in the middle of the lake, in the middle of the night!

> *But Jesus immediately said to them: "Take courage! It is I. Don't be afraid."*
>
> *"Lord, if it's you," Peter replied, "tell me to come to you on the water."*
>
> *"Come," he said.* (I bet Peter wasn't expecting Jesus to say that!)
>
> *Then Peter got down out of the boat, walked on the water and came toward Jesus.* **(Faith)**
>
> *But when he saw the wind, he was afraid and, beginning to sink, cried out, "Lord save me!"* **(Doubt)**
>
> *Immediately Jesus reached out his hand and caught him. "You of little faith," he said, "why did you doubt?"* **(God's grace)**
>
> *And when they climbed into the boat the wind died down. Then those who were in the boat worshiped him, saying, "Truly you are the Son of God." Matthew 14:25-33*

I think Jesus was thrilled to see that Peter wanted to step out in faith and He honors him by allowing him to walk on the water too! But Jesus uses the moment to teach a valuable lesson about faith. When you take your eyes off Jesus, you will begin to sink. If we look to anything or anyone other than God for our help (ourselves included), we will begin to sink, but Jesus is always right there to lift us up in a time of need, to save us. Notice in the story that Jesus never moved, He was always there. We need to remember it is us who can lose sight of Jesus, not the other way around. God hasn't left you or turned a "deaf" ear to you. He will not forsake those whom He has made a covenant with.

We are human and we will always have times when we lose sight of God and sink in our faith, but God is faithful. As God moves in our lives and our relationship with Him develops, we need to record his faithfulness so we won't forget. Even in the Old Testament, people were reminded to tell their children of God's faithfulness daily because God knows how quickly we can forget when hard times come.

> *Fix these words of mine in your hearts and minds; tie them as symbols on your hands and bind them on your foreheads. Teach them to your children, talking about them when you sit at home and when you walk along the road, when you lie down and when you get up. Deuteronomy 11:18*

We need to record those times when God comes through for us, the miracles, the healings and the times where everything turns out right at the last minute. We need to talk about the times when God has shown His faithfulness to us; How He has remained true to His word. When God moves, at the time, we think, "I'll never forget" but, as with all miracles, the vividness fades. Think about the most amazing experiences of your life; maybe a wedding, the birth of a child, a graduation or a mountain top experience. How clear are the details now?

We remember the event but forget many of the amazing details that happened during that time. It is these memories and recollections which sustain us during the times when we may not see God or His purposes so clearly. They keep us going until we can again say, "My God is faithful. He will never leave me nor forsake me." We can encourage each other until the fog fades and we see clearly that God really does hold true to His covenant with us.

What if I don't have anything to write or record?

If you have never had a relationship with Christ or are just beginning a journey with Him and have yet to experience His faithfulness, then you can read about His faithfulness to his covenants throughout the Bible. For the moment, to save you from trying to read the whole Bible to find them, I have covered some major covenants in the next chapter.

Notice that in each of these stories a step of faith led to an amazing God experience.

Chapter 7
Covenants of the Bible
So what's following God look like?

*Let this be written for a future generation
that a people not yet created may praise the Lord.*
Psalm 102:18

Our God has always been a God of covenants, even from the beginning of our recorded history. God made many covenants with His people and He remained faithful to them every time, even when they didn't. We can read of these accounts all through the Bible and be encouraged that God will always be faithful to His covenant with us even when we mess up or don't understand His ways.

The reason I love reading the stories of these covenants, between God and His people, is because they remind me that God immensely blessed those who were willing to face their fears, be obedient to God's call even if it meant doing "crazy" and "unthinkable" actions. They stood out in history because they were willing to be completely different from the society around them. There is a reason these stories have been recorded and shared throughout the centuries.

God still desires to be in a covenant with us today. That's what is so exciting about following Jesus, life goes beyond what you could ever imagine. You don't have to know everything about God and His word, He will guide you each step of the way as you begin to trust Him. He will put the path under your feet as you step into the unknown.
The people in this chapter were real people, like you and me. Every person had to take an immense step of faith yet God proved Himself over and over, throughout history. He will do the same for

you today. Try to imagine what it would be like if you were in the following stories. How would you respond to the calling of God?

NOAH

In Genesis, the very first book of the Bible, we find an example of one of the first covenants of the Bible. God says to Noah and his family,

> So God said to Noah, ' I am going to put an end to all people, for the earth is filled with violence because of them. I am surely going to destroy both them and the earth.
>
> So make yourself an ark of cypress wood...I am going to bring floodwaters on the earth to destroy all life under the heavens, every creature that has the breath of life in it. Everything on earth will perish. But I will establish my covenant with you, and you will enter the ark- you and your sons and your wife and your sons' wives with you.
>
> Noah did everything just as God commanded him.
>
> Genesis 6:13-18,22

What an intense statement from God. I'm sure there was confusion and fear within Noah and his family as they contemplated what the Lord was about to do around them and for them.

Here God says that He will establish His covenant with Noah and his family. However, it is only *after* Noah and his family enter that boat on faith and come out the other side that He actually establishes the covenant in such a way that proves to Noah He was faithful to His word.

From God's point of view, the covenant was truly established as soon as God spoke it for God never goes back on His word; so when He says I will establish a covenant, it is already done.

However, from Noah's point of view, he had to take God at His word and build an ark, round up the animals whilst enduring the ridicule of everyone around him. After ushering in a boatload of animals, he had to get on that ark with his family, in faith that God was going to do what He said He would. This is all before there was even a hint of a rain.

Imagine if God came to you today and asked you to build an ark. How would you respond?

The word tells us that it was about 120 years from the time that God initiated this covenant to the time it was fulfilled. Within that time, Noah had three children. They grew into adults and eventually married before work on the boat began. Building the ark is estimated to have taken anywhere between 55 to 75 years! Can you imagine being faithful for that amount of time when there is no support, but only ridicule, from the community around you?

It was after Noah's family got off the ark that God, in essence, proved His covenant in such a way that Noah could see it. After what I can only imagine being a wild boat ride, I'm sure Noah and his family wondered at times if they might perish in the flood too. They certainly would question when or if they would ever see land again. Yet, in Genesis 8:18, Noah came out of the boat, together with his family. God says to him,

> *I now establish my covenant with you and with your descendants after you and with every living creature that was with you...every living creature on earth. I establish my covenant with you: Never again will all life be cut off by the waters of a flood; never again will there be a flood to destroy the earth." And God said, "This is the sign of the covenant I am making with you, a covenant for all*

> *generations to come: I have set my rainbow in the clouds, and it will be the sign of the covenant between me and the earth.*
>
> Genesis 9:9

The story of the flood is told all over the world, in many different cultures and in many different ways. Sometimes because of its familiarity, we forget the detail of the tremendous amount of faith it took on behalf of Noah and his family.

ABRAHAM & SARAH

In Genesis 17, we find another covenant being made when God appeared to Abraham.

> *I am God Almighty, walk before me and be blameless. I will confirm my covenant between me and you and will greatly increase your numbers. Genesis 17:1-2*

Now if you don't know the story of Abraham, it is truly worth reading but to summarize, Abraham was a man who heard God and obeyed, most of the time. I like Abraham because when you read about him you see his human nature and all its flaws. The covenant that God had established with Abraham naturally required that Sarah, his wife, would conceive children in order to 'greatly increase' Abraham's numbers.

At 75 years of age, Abraham was called by God to leave his home to go to a new land. God promised to make him into a great nation. So he took his wife Sarah and they eventually find the new land. He doesn't stay there long due to a famine. So he visited Egypt for a time.

During this time Abraham, most likely filled with fear, decided to call his wife his sister so he would be treated well by the natives, who might want to marry her. He told Sarah not to tell anyone she was his wife.

Abraham got himself into quite a situation because, of all people, the Pharaoh became interested in his Sarah. He lavished upon Abraham sheep, cattle, donkeys, camels and even hired servants to wait upon him. The text is not clear on whether he aimed to take Sarah as his wife or in fact, did take her as his wife. Either way, Pharaoh's household experienced plagues because of his unknown sin. If the story ended there, God's covenant would not have been fulfilled. Pharaoh finds out Sarah is Abraham's wife, becomes furious and sends Abraham and his wife away with everything they had acquired.

Abraham then embarked on a lengthy and risky rescue mission for his nephew, Lot. Much time had passed. Abraham and Sarah were getting older and Sarah had still not conceived. Abraham began to doubt God's Covenant promise, so God reminded Abraham again of His promise to make Abraham into a great nation. And this time Abraham believes Him.

Unfortunately, Sarah began to doubt and came up with a plan of her own. She encouraged Abraham to sleep with her servant girl in an attempt to help God fulfill His plan. Well, they had a child all right, but all was not well. Sarah learned that her way brought jealousy and anger. She was angry and abused her servant so her servant ran away with Abraham's first son.

The Lord, once again, makes it clear to both Abraham and Sarah that he will start a nation through them. Sarah was now in her late eighties!

Here again, the covenant was established before Abraham (or Sarah) saw the proof. At a time that giving birth to a child would seem ridiculous and beyond all comprehension, Sarah, at 90 years of age, conceived and gave birth to her first child!
Notice even in their doubts and failures, God remained faithful to His covenant with Abraham and Sarah. Yes, they made mistakes and doubted, yet they kept returning to God. Notice that when they turned away from God's plan, there were many

uncomfortable consequences to their bad choices, yet there was always an opportunity to get up and try again.

How would you have responded? Would you have been faithful if you didn't see proof of God's word until you turned 90? Would you try to "help" God fulfill what He has promised you or would you have faith that God would stick by His word?

PHINEHAS

Sometimes God is so moved by a person stepping out in faith that He makes a covenant of blessing as a reward as seen in this passage:

> *The Lord said to Moses, 'Phinehas... has turned my anger away from the Israelites; for he was as zealous as I am for my honor among them, so that in my zeal I did not put an end to them. Therefore tell him I am making my covenant of peace with him. He and his descendants will have a covenant of a lasting priesthood, because he was zealous for the honor of his God and made atonement for the Israelites. Numbers 25:10-13*

The backdrop to this story is that the Holy people of God had begun to indulge in sexual sin with people who worshipped pagan gods. They not only were sexually immoral but worshipped these gods, yoking their very souls to evil. God saw it and wanted it to stop. A plague came upon the people in their sin.

Even the leaders were entwined in this sin. Balaam, a leader who spoke the word of God and had just blessed the nation of Israel, was one of the main perpetrators. It was his counsel that caused the Israelites to act treacherously against the LORD. The Lord was so angry that He commanded Moses to put all of the leaders of Israel to death in front of the people.

Moses was in the midst of this process when he was interrupted.

> *Then an Israelite man brought into the camp a Midianite woman right before the eyes of Moses and the whole assembly of Israel while they were weeping at the entrance to the tent of meeting. When Phinehas son of Eleazar, the son of Aaron, the priest, saw this, he left the assembly, took a spear in his hand and followed the Israelite into the tent. He drove the spear into both of them, right through the Israelite man and into the woman's stomach. Then the plague against the Israelites was stopped; but those who died in the plague numbered 24,000.*
> *Numbers 25:6-9*

How unbelievably defiant was this man that he didn't even hesitate to sin, in broad daylight, in front of an entire camp of people mourning the death of their leaders. He brought one of the pagan women whom God just spoke against, into his tent! But no one moved to do anything about this blatant challenge against God, except Phinehas.

Phinehas was blessed for standing up for God when no one else would.

Would you be brave enough to stand against what you knew was wrong? Would you ever take a stand for God when everyone around you seems to be complacent with the way things are?

DAVID

God began his covenant with David when he was only a child.

> *The Lord said to Samuel, "How long will you mourn for Saul, since I have rejected him as king over Israel? Fill your horn with oil and be on your way; I am sending you to Jesse of Bethlehem. I have chosen one of his sons to be king. 1 Samuel 16:1*

God sent Samuel, a priest, prophet and judge, to anoint a new king from the family lineage of Jesse's house. Samuel went to the house and asked Jesse to line up all of his sons.

> *Jesse had seven of his sons pass before Samuel, but Samuel said to him, "The Lord has not chosen these." So he asked Jesse, "Are these all the sons you have?"*
>
> *"There is still the youngest," Jesse answered, "but he is tending the sheep." 1 Samuel 16:10-11*

David was the youngest and apparently, the least likely candidate to be anointed a king, according to his family. He didn't even get into the initial line up! But God had big plans for him even though he was so young. David was a faithful young man who knew how to look after and protect his sheep. God saw what no one else could see; that within this young boy was the making of a great King.

God led David throughout his life and never left his side. As David listened and obeyed, God extended his covenant.

> *I took you from the pasture, from tending the flock, and appointed you ruler over my people Israel. I have been with you wherever you have gone, and I have cut off all your enemies from before you. Now I will make your name great, like the names of the greatest men on earth.*
>
> *2 Samuel 7: 8-9*

God's covenant finished with an eternal promise.

> *Your house and your kingdom will endure forever before me; your throne will be established forever. 2 Samuel 7:16*

There are many examples of David's faith in God but one of my favorite stories was when David, still a young man, went out to defeat a giant who intimidated the entire army of Israel. (1 Samuel 17).

When David volunteered to slay the giant, the men just laughed at him. David was so angry that anyone would dare question God's faithfulness that, armed with only his slingshot and a stone, he took aim and, with one strike, knocked the giant down.

David had more faith than the entire Israelite army! He knew God's covenant was to establish him as a king, so he couldn't lose. He knew God would protect him, so he boldly went out to fight a giant that intimidated everyone else.

Not only did God bless David with a victory in that battle but in many battles to come. God aligned him to be a King and not just any king. He was the king that many Biblical characters would be referred to as coming from "the line of David". Amazingly, this was the lineage that led to our Lord, Jesus Christ, the highest King of all! What a covenant!

David had many fears and went through tough times, yet he placed his trust in the Lord and was blessed immensely. When he messed up, he kept coming back to God. He had such self-confidence in the Lord, that he told God to "Keep me as the apple of your eye." Psalm 17:8.

David's story shows us that if we have full confidence in God, He will never let us down. We can step out and know God has our back. We can place our full trust in Him.

JESUS CHRIST

In the Old Testament, animals were sacrificed for the sins God's people had committed. Nearly the entire book of Leviticus talks about the various animals that were sacrificed for sins. I bring this up because these sacrifices help us to begin to understand the greatest covenant of all between God and humanity. These sacrifices served as a prophetical sign of what God was about to do through his son Jesus.

> *If he brings a lamb as his sin offering, he is to bring a female without defect. He is to lay his hand on its head and slaughter it for a sin offering... In this way the priest will make atonement for him for the sin he has committed, and he will be forgiven-*
> Leviticus 4:32- 35

When the people of the Old Testament wanted forgiveness of their sins, they would bring a perfect lamb, "without defect", to be sacrificed for their sins.

As an animal lover, I have a hard time reading this. I mean, what did the poor lamb do? Nothing! The lamb was perfect. Yet, it had to be sacrificed for the sins that mankind committed. Just knowing that fluffy little lamb was being held on the altar because of what I had done, would make me feel horrible. That alone would make me not want to sin anymore. Yet God would use that consequence of sin to help us understand more of who He is and what He would do for us because of His great love. That lamb would be symbolic of what God was about to do through his son Jesus.

When the Son of God became flesh, He was that perfect lamb. He was sinless, He did nothing wrong and history attests to this. No one has ever been able to pin anything on Jesus because he was flawless. He had to be so that He could be a "lamb without defect" sacrificed for all of our sins. He was crucified for our sins. What mankind did to Him is unspeakable. He died the cruelest of deaths taking the punishment of our sins.
After His death, animal sacrifices stopped because He fulfilled what they only symbolized. He took death upon himself because He knew we couldn't. He not only died for our sins, He defeated death. He didn't stay dead, He rose again and is alive now! We will never be able to fully appreciate what God has accomplished through Jesus, until the day we meet Him face to face.

Hebrews chapters 9 and 10 explain the meaning of the sacrifice of Jesus. I encourage you to read these chapters and ask God to help you understand just what He has done through the death and resurrection of Jesus Christ.

In the Old Testament times, a priest would go into the part of the worship tent called the "Holy of Holies" once a year to offer a blood sacrifice for his own sins and for the sins his nation's people had committed in ignorance. Again this would be symbolic of the blood that would be sacrificed through the death of Jesus. Blood signifies that Jesus, although God, became human. He became one of us. Blood is what flows throughout every part of our body bringing life; without it, we are dead.

In the New Testament, we have three accounts of Jesus speaking of a new covenant using the cup of communion.

> "Drink from it, all of you. This is my blood of the covenant, which is poured out for many for the forgiveness of sins."
> Matthew 26:28, Mark 14:24 and Luke 22:20

Jesus inferred the wine was symbolic of his own blood that was about to be spilled out for humanity. It was a symbol of what was about to happen.

Imagine being the very essence of God and trying to explain to your disciples what was about to happen. Jesus spoke symbolically to help us get a glimpse into the understanding of the divine.

Later in 1 Corinthians 11:17-33, Paul wrote that when we take communion it is to remember Jesus and this covenant and that our sins have been paid for. When we come to Jesus and ask His forgiveness, He receives our request for forgiveness and we are forgiven. Jesus took care of that penalty for us on the cross. We no longer have to carry around guilt and shame.

What is so amazing is that Christ's death and resurrection are current as well as historical. God is not bound by time like we are. Although, He created time for us so that we could cope with life. God is outside of time.

> *For a thousand years in your sight are like a day that has just gone by, or like a watch in the night- Psalm 90:4*

> *But do not forget this one thing, dear friends: With the Lord a day is like a thousand years, and a thousand years are like a day. 2 Peter 3:8*

So although historically Jesus died on a cross, He could see right through time to all of humanity at once.

It's as if He is looking at you right now on that cross, saying that you are loved and you are forgiven. He willingly takes the penalty for your sins and dies for you right now, so that you may find life. The covenant He makes with you is current. The covenant: He died so you may live. He has covered all your mistakes, broken laws, sin, guilt and shame, so you may live your life in freedom, with joy and contentment, forever.

> *The deliverer will come from Zion; he will turn godlessness away from Jacob. And this is my covenant with them when I take away their sins- Romans 11:26b-27.*

What does He ask in return?

> *Tell them this is what the Lord, the God of Israel, says: "Cursed is the man who does not obey the terms of my covenant- the terms I commanded your forefathers when I brought them out of Egypt, out of the iron-smelting furnace." I said, "Obey me and do everything I command you, and you will be my people, and I will*

> *be your God. Then I will fulfill the oath I swore to your forefathers, to give them a land flowing with milk and honey- the land you possess today- Jeremiah 11:3*

While this covenant was for the Old Testament Jews, the imagery is helpful for us to understand the new covenant under Jesus. The terms of the covenant God holds with us today is simple enough. He provides the land flowing with milk and honey. Although this passage refers to a place of the past, it also refers to the present and the future!

Let me explain. If you are reading this book, whether you realize it or not, you are currently in a land filled with milk and honey. A land where you have been provided for and a way made for you to live, not just to survive but to live and to live well. It's there surrounding you now but you'll have to separate yourself from the world's chaos to see it.

The world is loud. It interferes with God's peace. The world will have you running in circles leaving you exhausted. You'll be too busy to notice people that God has placed in your path and too much in a rush to slow down and hear His voice. You will have to draw away from the worldly way to experience the beauty of the land God has provided for you now.

There is another land of milk and honey yet to be experienced. God promises us that we may dwell with Him forever in this land one day if we commit to Him now. That land is perfect in every way and there will be no more sorrow or tears. It is a land that gives us hope when this life can seem meaningless.

So what are we to do in return?

Obey the Lord and do what He says! When you ask Jesus to be Lord of your life, you're asking for him to guide you and direct you so that you will be on the right path; the path that leads to freedom, joy and contentment; the path that leads to eternal life.

You are recognizing His authority over your life. He has paid for you with His life! When you enter that sacred covenant with Him you are choosing to give your life back to Him. He's had it all along but when we make a decision out of our own choice to truly hand our life over to him, it says, "I love you".

Christians are people who have given up on trying to run their own lives because they realize it leads nowhere. They had nothing but confusion, sorrow and discontentment on that path. So they have asked Jesus to be their Savior and to guide them on the path God has created for them. No one is able to follow God on his or her own, which is why we need Jesus to help us. Just look at the Old Testament, when people tried to follow God, their humanness won out and they made a mess of it every time! So they desperately called out for help and God sent Jesus.

We can't obey God without His help. When Jesus returned to heaven, He left us a helper called the Holy Spirit. He talks about this in the following passage,

> *If you love me, you will obey what I command. And I will ask the Father, and He will give you another Counselor to be with you forever- the Spirit of Truth. The world cannot accept him, because it neither sees him nor knows him. But you know him, for he lives with you and will be in you. I will not leave you as orphans; I will come to you- John 14:15-18*

The Holy Spirit is part of what is known as the Trinity. This concept is not so hard to understand when you look at how we are made up as human beings. We have a physical body, a mind and a spirit. God says that we are made in His image (Gen. 1:26-27) God is made up of the Father, the Son and the Holy Spirit. God is the mind (creator), Jesus is the flesh, and the Holy Spirit is really the way God communes with us in our spirit.

> On that day you will realize that I am in my Father, and you are in me, and I am in you - John 14:20

The Holy Spirit works within us guiding us to and along the narrow path of life that leads to truth, contentment and eternal life.

> Not that we are competent in ourselves to claim anything for ourselves, but our competence comes from God. He has made us competent as ministers of a new covenant- not of the letter but of the Spirit; for the letter kills, but the Spirit gives life.
> 2 Corinthians 3:5-6

So how about you? Would you be willing to take a step of faith to trust in the God who has never let His people down? Give your life to God to see what amazing things He could do with it!

> Jesus replied, "If anyone loves me, he will obey my teaching. My Father will love him, and we will come to him and make our home with him. John 14:23

> For God so loved the world that he gave his one and only Son, that whoever believes in him shall not perish but have eternal life. For God did not send His son to condemn the world, but to save the world through Him. John 3:16-17

God offers His covenant to you. He will forgive you, cleanse you from all the mistakes, offer you hope and a future. How will you respond to His covenant with you?

Chapter 8
Hearing from God
Does God really speak to people?

"If anyone hears my voice and opens the door, I will come in..."
Revelation 3:20

I could feel the stress building up in me over the week. I got to the weekend and my teenage son, unbeknownst to him, pulled the last straw that was holding all of my sanity and calmness together. Thankfully, he left the house to go to school before I unloaded. The poor thing just happened to be the last one to cross the bridge before the dam burst. He didn't do anything really horrible; it was a simple issue of not doing a couple of his chores around the house.

Normally, I allow some grace, as he is a hard-working, studying student. But add 3 other children who are not pulling their weight in chores and a family who has become lazy, leaving things around the house everywhere, well something opened up in me. It took something this simple to go deep within me and suddenly, things I didn't even know I was harboring in there, came forth. I was mad, angry and I let everyone know it. It was not a pretty sight!

I felt like a slave to those living around me. When I asked anyone to do anything for me, the grunting and moaning mixed with a poor attitude, made me feel like I was always the "bad guy" of the family. Funny enough, no one ever simply volunteered to help me around the house because they felt grateful to be a part of the family. It was always me having to ask everyone to do what complete strangers would do out of respect for another person.

"Can you move your shoes from out of the doorway and put them into your room?

"Can you not leave your sticky jam covered bowl on the couch?"

"Would you possibly be able to wipe the piles of hair off the bathroom counter after you have brushed your hair?" and so on.

I felt resentful and stuck in a place I didn't want to be. I remembered the long-ago dreams of what I wanted to do with my life and, funny enough, none of them involved being a slave to those who lived in my house. Would it kill someone to smile occasionally and maybe offer a "Thank you Mom for all you do for me?"

Now I'm sure most of you can relate to my feelings even if you're in a different situation. Maybe you had a long day at work followed by a traffic jam. It could be you had a disagreement with a spouse or a parent. It could be some sort of project that failed. We all have people or situations which can bring us to this point where we are just fed up with life in general. When I'm in this place I feel so ugly inside. Deep down, I don't want to be this way, but the defense lawyer who resides within me doesn't want to let it go, and, in the end, I find I just don't have it in me to change and be the better person.

I could have easily stayed in this place harboring a lot of bitter resentment, grumping around and feeling perfectly justified. But fortunately, I recognized the signs, the signs of fatigue, hopelessness and defeat. These are all signs that I needed to have what I call 'soul rest'. I needed to escape from my home and meet with my Father.

> *Very early in the morning, while it was still dark, Jesus got up, left the house and went off to a solitary place, where he prayed. Simon and his companions went to look for him, and when they found him they exclaimed: "Everyone is looking for you!" Mark 1:35-37*

In my mind, I can almost hear Jesus reply, "I know".

I'm positive He knew what it felt like when everyone wants a piece of you and you are running out of energy. When there is no "you" left to give.

I knew, unfortunately from experience, that at this time I crucially needed to refill or I would head towards serious burnout and slide into depression or despair. Things can quickly spiral downwards when one doesn't get enough refueling time with God.

Instead of continuing my self-pity party, I decided I would set some time aside to meet with God. So the next morning, I sent the kids away with their father and I went out to meet with mine. What I needed was one on one, uninterrupted time with Jesus, away from others. I needed to hear His take on life and gain some wisdom. I needed the peace that only He can give.

As I walked, I felt some of the pent up steam evaporating with each step. I went down to the beach and watched the rhythm of the waves. The sun was out and the temperature was cool and fresh. The air was so clean. I breathed it in large, deep breaths. I heard the crickets in the bushes behind me chirp out the tempo of life.

Wow, I hadn't heard crickets in a long time. It had been too long since the last soul rest.

Why do I wait until my life is falling apart before I take the time I so desperately need with my Father?

I sat down with my Bible and my notebook and began to pray. As I prayed, God began to unravel the twisted threads of my soul that I had so easily knotted up with the stresses of my life. I graciously received all that He had to give. My soul began to experience the peace it had been crying out for.

Our body needs physical rest but our spirit needs soul rest. They are two completely different kinds of rest and we need both. In the physical, the body will eventually force itself to shut down and we will get rest. In the spiritual, we have to force our mind to shut down so that the Holy Spirit can do his work in our soul. It is in this state of rest that we will hear the voice of God speaking into our life.

I didn't always know how to recognize my need for soul rest nor did I understand how much God wanted to speak to me. I thought He only spoke to certain people, like prophets and preachers. Although I felt I heard God occasionally, I was always left wondering if it was really God or my imagination. I wanted more from God. I wanted to know God and hear His voice.

God first answered my desire at an Easter Camp. The speaker in the morning session encouraged us to find somewhere to be still and not to leave that place until we heard God. I had nowhere else to be, so I took up the challenge.

I went to the beach and began to wait. An hour went by and I found that I had spent the whole time just running the movie reels of the past week's events over and over in my head. I thought about all the things I had and hadn't done. I thought about the conversation I overheard in the toilets about a close friend of mine. I thought of the things around the house that needed repair.

"Oh, focus, focus! You're here to listen to God, not daydream!" I chastised myself.

Another hour went by and I found that memories from my childhood were popping into my head. I jerked my brain back into focus.

Another hour went by, and I found that I was mesmerized by the scenery around me. I just love the beach.

"Not again! Focus!"

As the next hour slowly ticked by, I felt my body hurting. I had been sitting too long in one place. I got up and stretched and moved around. I was then distracted by all of the aches in my body. A twinge in the neck brought about questions of how long that had been going on. My shoulders ached. I remembered the swimming accident I had had years ago that left me on the couch taking painkillers for weeks. My sinuses were half blocked and I thought about the yellow-flowered tree that brought on most of my sinus problems. Then I yelled at myself. "How am I ever going to hear God if I can't clear my head of all this junk? Lord, help me!"

As the hours moved forward, my mind began to calm down and I remembered the story of Elijah.

> The Lord said, "Go out and stand on the mountain in the presence of the Lord, for the Lord is about to pass by."
>
> Then a great and powerful wind tore the mountains apart and shattered the rocks before the Lord, but the Lord was not in the wind. After the wind there was an earthquake, but the Lord was not in the earthquake. After the earthquake came a fire, but the Lord was not in the fire. And after the fire came a gentle whisper. When Elijah heard it, he pulled his cloak over his face and went out and stood at the mouth of the cave.
>
> Then a voice said to him, "What are you doing here, Elijah?"
>
> 1 Kings 19:11-13

Finally, it became quiet around me and, more importantly, within me. I began to hear the Lord speak. It was as if He spoke divine information including the feelings of peace and assurance, as well as visions, into an instant download within my heart. It is quite difficult to describe and I imagine His voice sounds unique to each individual. I know some people actually hear God audibly. I didn't hear an audible voice but it was a voice in my thoughts. It seemed to speak not only to my brain but also to my heart. The information was simply there all at once like I had a memory of someone saying it earlier. I had no doubt about what I learned. It was if it had already happened. And because God is outside of time, I imagine it did.

I say this cautiously because this is the way God spoke to me. As I said earlier, He speaks differently to every person so do not lock my experience into your expectation when you go and meet with God.

I took that experience home with me. The more I heard from God, the more I wanted to hear. I wanted to know Him. It was like falling in love for the first time. I wanted to spend every moment getting to know God more. I was so amazed at what He was teaching me. The only thing that kept getting in the way was life and all of its "busy" ness!

A couple of months after the Easter camp, my husband and I decided to go on a weekend Prayer Retreat. It was to be a retreat about hearing God. At first, I was hesitant to go because I was so exhausted at the time. I kept thinking to myself, "I hope they don't fill up the weekend with classes and activities! I just want a bit of time to myself to rest. I'm so tired, I just want to sleep!"

To my utter amazement, they only spoke to us the night we arrived for about 45 minutes. We spent the rest of the weekend just waiting on God and listening. I had never spent a whole weekend just waiting for God to speak to me. Afterward, I wondered why we didn't do this every month. It was the best experience I've ever had. It locked in the reality of my relationship with God and opened a whole new perspective of Christianity to me. What I gleaned from that weekend kept teaching me things for months. It went beyond what I was receiving from my daily time of reading and praying yet afterward, it made those times more powerful and clear.

A couple of years later, an opportunity arose that allowed me to have one free day a week. I took that day to simply go out and wait on God. It was the best year of my life. So many dreams became a reality that year. I learned many skills that would help me later in life when I wouldn't have the advantage of having the time to go and be still for an entire day each week.

What I'm trying to get across to you is that if you want to hear from God, you need to do two things: make the time (schedule it in) and be still. This runs contrary to everything that our world thrives on; rushing around and being busy.

Now I know it is difficult to make this sort of time with God but believe me, it is worth the effort. I believe that actively seeking God at every opportunity allows the communication lines to open. Yet I cannot take credit for actively seeking Him. Even that was a result of asking God not only for the opportunity to meet with Him but for strength to put aside my will so that His would prevail. I freely admit I just don't have it naturally within me to do the will of God. I have to ask God to help me to care enough to make the effort to meet with Him.

Sometimes people say to me, "Oh, you're so obedient to God." And I laugh. If other people saw the movie reel of God calling me to spend time with Him, they definitely would not admire my kind of obedience. Don't get me wrong, I get there in the end but there is a whole lot of ugly before then. There are arguments, excuses, whining and moaning sessions, especially when He tries to wake me early in the morning. But when I do finally wake up and meet with Him, I keep asking Him to persevere with me because I always leave our times together a happier and better person.

If you want to hear from God, ask Him for the strength to help you put aside time to meet with Him. Don't worry about how it looks.

There's nothing He hasn't experienced before. He wants to communicate with you.

It reminds me of my cross-country running days, as short-lived as they were. I hated running yet when I finished a run, I loved it. When it was time to run, I would come up with every excuse not to run, but once I was on the track and going, despite my feelings, I slowly came around to enjoying it. I finished feeling healthier and more energized for the day. Coming to God is very similar.

When you do finally make a plan to meet with God, I can tell you now that at least ten other things will try and get in the way. There will be unexpected visitors, a call into work or an emergency of some kind or another. Then there will be the practicality problems. You will think you need to accomplish a hundred other tasks before you can meet with God. The laundry will suddenly need to be done and even though you have never ironed before, today it will seem critical. A dripping tap will suddenly alert you that you need to change all of the washers in the house or a glance outside will remind you that you need to mow the lawn. All sorts of things will stand in the way, but if you ask God to help you, He will. He wants us to know that we can't do anything without His help.

> *I am the vine; you are the branches. If a man remains in me and I in him, he will bear much fruit; apart from me you can do nothing. If anyone does not remain in me, he is like a branch that is thrown away and withers; such branches are picked up, thrown in the fire and burned. If you remain in me and my words remain in you, ask whatever you wish, and it will be given you. This is to my Father's glory, that you bear much fruit, showing yourselves to be my disciples. John 15:5-8.*

If you do make time to meet with God and you get interrupted or distracted, don't give up. If you feel like you are not hearing from God when you have made the time, don't give up. If nothing seems to be going the way you thought, don't give up! It's okay if you don't get it right; don't feel like a failure. Just ask again. Don't stop asking God to help you. He loves persistence. You'll find He will give you just what you need in order to hear him.

> *If any of you lacks wisdom, he should ask God, who gives generously to all without finding fault, and it will be given to him. But when he asks, he must believe and not doubt, because he who doubts is like a wave of the sea, blown and tossed by the wind.*
> James 1:5-7

There are a couple of things I want to mention that will help get you to the point of hearing God faster.

First, you have to be open and willing to change, willing to hear the truth and let go of the stuff that you think you need. It's a bit like decluttering or minimizing your mind and soul. Confess your mistakes and your sin. Don't harbor sin in your life. We all have sin in our lives but to harbor sin is like growing a crop of mushrooms; keep them in the dark and feed them feces. Sin is kept alive by justifying it and keeping it in the dark. Sin is fed by continually thinking about what is equivalent to spiritual feces. The last thing that you want is to bring your sin out of the dark recesses of your life into the light of God where He can fix it. But it needs to be done. Be willing to admit you're wrong and open yourself to change.

Secondly, you need to be reading God's word, the Bible, as much as you can. This will help you to recognize any sin you may be harboring, but it is also a basis from which God will work. God will never say anything contrary to His word. Don't simply trust what other people tell you about God, check it out for yourself!

The more you feed your mind with the word of God, the more the Holy Spirit has to work with. It will enable God to speak more quickly with you because you are on the same page, so to speak.

> *My son, if you accept my words and store up my commands within you, turning your ear to wisdom and applying your heart to understanding, and if you call out for insight and cry aloud for understanding, and if you look for it as for silver and search for it as for hidden treasure, then you will understand the fear of the Lord and find the knowledge of God. Proverbs 2:1-5*

> *For the Lord gives wisdom, and from his mouth come knowledge and understanding. Proverbs 2:6*

Let me give you an example of how God uses His word to speak to me. Let's say that I open my Bible in the morning and I read the following passage from Ephesians,

> *Be kind and compassionate to one another, forgiving each other, just as in Christ God forgave you. Ephesians 4:32*

Then in the afternoon while I'm in the grocery store, a woman with a full cart of groceries races in front of me to the "express" lane, where you are only supposed to have 12 items or less. I'm in a bit of a rush and a little frustrated that she seems oblivious to the number of people lining up behind her now. Although she is finished, after what seemed like an eternity, she is now slowly putting her money away in her purse and checking her receipt to make sure it is correct.

I want to shout, "Move out of the way lady!! Can't you see it is the express lane and you've already taken forever?" But then the Holy Spirit brings the verse from this morning into my mind. My arms start to move the cart forward to gently nudge her out of the way, but suddenly a conviction arises within me to have compassion. I hear the people behind me saying negative comments to her but I feel the need to encourage her.

Where is this coming from? I know God is speaking to me because of two reasons; one, it is so unlike me, and two, it is Biblical.

If I hadn't read the Bible verse this morning, the Holy Spirit couldn't bring it into my mind. He wouldn't have had anything to work with. But since the word went into my mind, He simply had to bring it to the forefront at the right time and use it to teach me.

With the help of the Holy Spirit, I was able to see the "express lane" woman in the way God sees her, with compassion and love. If I were able to see into her life with God's looking glass, I might have been able to see a woman struggling to feed her family after the loss of her husband. A woman trying her best to get by each day, but living in such a haze she doesn't even notice when she is in the wrong lane. Hopefully, by smiling and offering a word of encouragement, I was able to impart something kind and uplifting into her soul that day.

Finally, if you want to hear God faster, you have to make the time. You just have to make it happen. If one of your family members went to the hospital, you would make the time to go see them. If you loved someone and they needed time with you, you would make the time, simple enough.

This is a call to meet with your Creator, who also happened to create everything around you. Do I even need to say that it's a priority? How much do you love your Savior? You need to schedule it in and give that time solely to God. That means you leave anyplace you may be distracted and go somewhere you will not be disturbed. You'll need to leave your mobile at home (or at least turn it off), take your Bible, pen and paper and plan to be gone for at least a couple of hours. Why not make a day of it?

Chapter 9
Listen!
Why am I not hearing anything?

He who belongs to God hears what God says...
John 8:47

I want to share with you a very special passage of God's word:

> Hear, O Israel: The Lord our God, the Lord is one. Love the Lord with all your heart and with all your soul and with all your strength. These commandments that I give you today are to be on your hearts.   Deuteronomy 6:4-6

This is the beginning of a huge passage. The first two words of this passage, 'Sh'ma Yisrael', translated,

> "Hear O Israel, The Lord is our God. The Lord is one."

is the centerpiece of the Jewish morning and evening prayers. It is considered the most important part of the prayer session and is prayed twice daily. They teach their children to say it before they go to bed each night. Jesus emphasizes it in the New Testament,

> The most important one (commandment)," answered Jesus, "is this: 'Hear, O Israel: The Lord is one. Love the Lord your God with all your heart and with all your soul and with all your strength.' The second is this: 'Love your neighbor as yourself." There is no commandment greater than these.   Mark 12:29

So often when I read the Bible I see that God speaks in circles. God is infinite in all directions and everything begins and ends in Him. He is the beginning and the end wrapped up in one.

I am the Alpha and Omega, the First and the Last, the Beginning and the End. Rev. 22:13

Many times He will begin passages with the end result and vice versa. Notice that the Sh'ma starts with a keyword, "**Hear**!" Yes, He is commanding his people to hear what He is saying and at the same time declaring that by doing what He says, "love the Lord with all your heart, soul and mind", they will hear. It's a circle. It's like the passages that start with "Blessed is he who...," God gives the blessing first but you have to obey the words that follow to receive the blessing.[3]

God wants His people to hear him. In fact, He is commanding it. The word 'Hear' is imperative here. It is a command. Yet what follows in the passage will need to be accomplished to truly hear. If we want to hear God speak we need to be in the moment with all our heart, soul and strength.

Is that how you come to God in prayer? How important is this time to you?

The passage emphasizes that His commandments are to be on your heart all the time. These commands are the things God wants you to think about, obsess about if you will, all the time. He doesn't want you to focus on the reruns of all the hurt someone has caused you or the jealousy over someone else's talents and gifts. He's got better things for you to think about. A lighter way to live life, without carrying the burdens of our sinful nature.

The passage goes on to say that we are to talk about God's commands.

---

[3] See Jeremiah 17:7-8, Psalm 1:1, Matthew 5:3-12, Psalm 31:1-2

> *Teach them to your children, talking about them when you sit at home and when you walk along the road, when you lie down and when you get up. Deuteronomy 11:19*

This means we are to talk about the Bible and the direction God is leading us in life. This is what He wants us to talk about with our children.

How often do you speak about life and spiritual issues with your family? What consumes most of your conversations in general? What do your conversations look like if you are having them at all? If you are not continually thinking about it, the "busy" ness of life will drive out these all-important conversations. If you tend to be forgetful, like me, write down the passages of the Bible that move you and seemingly speak just to you!

> *Write them on the door frames of your houses and on your gates. Deuteronomy 6:8*

Granted this may be in the form of sticky notes! Do whatever it takes to get His word into your life.

I love the series, The Chronicles of Narnia by C.S. Lewis. One of my favorite parts is when Aslan (symbolic of Christ) tells Lucy to repeat what he said every day so she will not forget his commands. As time passes and life gets busy, the repetition slips slowly away. Then suddenly she finds she is in the place she was forewarned about and she can't remember a thing he had told her.

Life can easily move what seems a powerful message from God to something that we heard once so long ago we've forgotten what was said.

> *When the Lord brings you into the land....a land with large, flourishing cities you did not build, houses filled with all kinds of good things you did not provide, wells you did not dig and vineyards and olives you did not plant- then when you eat and are satisfied, be careful that you do not forget the Lord, who brought you out of Egypt, out of the land of slavery.*
> Deuteronomy 6:10-12

When God provides you with opportunities and blessings that you had no hand in, be thankful and do not forget God. We tend to take a lot for granted. We are surrounded by blessings that we had no part of making but yet benefit from. Take some of the simple things like electricity, clean water, fresh food at a local grocer, cars, easily accessible gasoline for those cars, heating, air-conditioning and modern medicine. Most of which none of us had a hand in creating but are able to use today. Spiritually, we are even more blessed. We have God's word in about a thousand different translations, computer access to all sorts of teaching on God's word and local churches on call in just about every city.

I find that just about every passage in the Bible that speaks about hearing God and understanding His will for your life will also have a teaching on humility. Here He reminds His people they had nothing to do with their blessings. There is no room for any pride or arrogance when all has been provided for you. They were, as we are, completely dependent on God, whether we like to admit it or not.

> *The brother in humble circumstances ought to take pride in his high position. But the one who is rich should take pride in his low position, because he will pass away like a wild flower.*
> James 1:9-10

Another great verse for determining the will of God in our lives is from the book of Romans.

> *Therefore, I urge you, brothers, in view of God's mercy, to offer your bodies as living sacrifices, holy and pleasing to God- this is your spiritual act of worship. Do not conform any longer to the pattern of this world, but be transformed by the renewing of your mind. Then you will be able to test and approve what God's will is- his good, pleasing and perfect will.   Romans 12:1-2*

Here again, it stresses submission to God. If you are not ready to offer yourself completely to God, then what is the point of asking what His will is for your life?

A living sacrifice means that when God asks, you are willing to lay down your life for Him and do what He asks. He doesn't want you to literally die on an altar. You are a "living" sacrifice. When He speaks, you will receive such peace in your life. You'll feel refreshed, empowered to do great things, whatever they may be. You will feel more alive than you ever have.

If you look again, this verse tells us to not conform any longer to the pattern of this world.

What does the pattern of this world teach us? To strive and to achieve whatever you want. You are in charge of your life. Who cares who you step on to get what you need or want? Bend the rules a little to accommodate your needs. Hide the truth. Take the short cut. Superficial beauty and strength is everything. Get more, spend more, achieve more, want more.

It's a never-ending circle. We have to cut ourselves off from the world and get away to hear the voice of God. When we do we will know God's will for us and be able to give it a test run. Again, straight after this teaching, we are reminded to remain humble.

> *For by the grace given me I say to every one of you: Do not think of yourself more highly than you ought, but rather think of*

> *yourself with sober judgment, in accordance with the measure of faith God has given you. Romans 12:3*

Finally, I want to look at a hard-core teaching that Jesus presented to the Jews in the New Testament.

> *He who belongs to God hears what God says. The reason you do not hear is that you do not belong to God. John 8:47*

Jesus was talking to the Jews here. Out of all the people in the world, the Jews were known to belong to God. How could Jesus say to "God's chosen people" that they did not belong to God? This was such an offensive statement to make and it still is. This is the type of statement that starts wars. The truth can do that. Jesus looked into their souls to the state of their hearts and all was not well. The reason He knew they didn't belong to God is that they were not hearing Him. They had closed their ears.

The Jews were basing their righteousness on *their* understanding of God's word. Their understanding was greatly influenced by customs and traditions that had accumulated over time. Somewhere along the way, they had forgotten to check with God that they were still on the right track. They had become set in their ways and in their thinking, and pride started to creep in.

> *The way of a fool seems right to him, but a wise man overlooks an insult. A fool shows his annoyance at once but a prudent man overlooks an insult. Proverbs 12:15*

When we are convinced our way is the best way, we can be quick to make it the only way, judging others for not thinking the same. When someone tells us something contrary to our own belief, we can be quick to dismiss them and continue on our way, even if God himself is telling us we are wrong. Many times we get offended that someone thinks differently to us. We are offended that God would call our sin what it is. But God wants us to remain humble and have the capacity to admit when we are wrong. We can only do this when we have the right attitude in our hearts. It is the state of our heart that is so important to God. It is within our hearts that we will become more like Jesus.

Why does God want us to be like Jesus? Jesus is equivalent to life, true life and life in all its fulness. He is truth and love combined. When we become like Jesus, we begin to understand what we were originally designed for in all of its glory and goodness. Jesus is the baseline of what freedom was designed to be. He was unmoved by the world or Satan. He held the power of God and used it to help and heal others. Although Satan threw everything at Him, nothing moved Him from His original plan and He did everything at the right time. Much to the frustration of others, Jesus had perfect timing. He knew what His purpose was, where He was going and how it would all turn out. He was not afraid of death because He knew death had no power over Him.

God holds the answers to this life, yet, He will always allow us the freedom to follow Him or to go our own way. I've tried my own way and ended up in a very big mess. How's your own way going? I want to encourage you to say, "I give up" and literally give up your way of doing things and ask God for a better way. This will open the door to a better way of life. Forcibly slowing down your life to listen to God will enable you to do that life with someone who loves you more than you could ever imagine.

Chapter 10
What I Heard
What does God say when He speaks?

See, the former things have taken place, and new things I declare; before they spring into being I announce them to you.
Isaiah 42:9

People are often surprised when I say that I hear God speak to me. They wonder what He sounds like and what He says, so I wanted to share some of my personal experiences to show how God has interacted with me at various times in my life.

My Father

A couple of years ago, my Father planned to have knee surgery. He had put it off for years because of the time and cost of the procedure. It eventually got so bad that he couldn't get up and down the steps anymore or walk any further than his driveway without pain.

When he went in for pre-surgery testing on his knee, they found an unexpected surprise, a large portion of the aorta leading to his heart was blocked. He was booked in for immediate heart surgery. This was a shock to us all and we had people everywhere praying for him. As I prayed for him I opened my Bible to the book of Isaiah. I felt the following passages jump off the page and into my heart.

> *For I am the Lord, your God, who takes hold of your right hand and says to you, "Do not fear; I will help you. Do not be afraid, O worm Jacob, O little Israel, for I myself will help you," declares*

the Lord. See I will make you into a threshing sledge, new and sharp, with many teeth. You will thresh the mountains and crush them, and reduce the hills to chaff...but you will rejoice in the Lord and glory in the Holy One of Israel.

I, the Lord, have called you in righteousness; I will take hold of your hand. I will keep you and will make you to be a covenant for the people and a light for the Gentiles, to open eyes that are blind, to free captives from prison and to release from the dungeon those who sit in darkness. I am the Lord; that is my name! I will not give my glory to another or my praise to idols. See, the former things have taken place, and new things I declare; before they spring into being I announce them to you.
Isaiah 41:13-16 and 42:6-7

God assured me that all would be fine in this surgery and that my Father would come out of it giving more glory to God than ever before. I knew that God would use him and his circumstance to encourage others and bring them into a closer relationship with God.

Before he went in to have the surgery, I Skyped Dad and read the passage to him. He chuckled and said God had been taking him through the book of Isaiah and encouraging him with the exact same passage. We prayed together and would not chat again until after the surgery a couple of days later.

Well, the operation went well but the medical staff gave him the wrong medication which set him back greatly. He was forced to stay in the hospital for six weeks to recover.

When we talked again, he expressed that although he was frustrated being stuck in the hospital, God used his situation in amazing ways.

The pastor from Dad's church had come in to visit Dad, and as the pastor headed towards Dad's room, he ran into another member from his church who explained he was visiting a family member who had been given only a few hours to live. She was frightened of dying. The pastor stopped to pray with her and led that young lady into a relationship with Jesus. She no longer feared death. The pastor told my Dad that if he had not stayed in the hospital for as long as he did, that young lady might have never known God's peace.

As the pastor left that day, he was told that the young lady had gone to be with the Lord. That story so encouraged my father it made him cry.

Eventually, Dad left the hospital and began his long journey of rehabilitation. This was very difficult as the medical staff wanted Dad to walk around but because he never had knee surgery, he could barely walk. But if he didn't walk his heart wouldn't get stronger so that he could eventually have the knee surgery. It was a very difficult and frustrating time for him, but he was so thankful to be alive and experiencing so much more intimacy with his God.

After a few weeks at home, my dad and step-mother decided that with winter and snow coming to Indiana, where they lived, they would head to Florida for a couple of weeks to help Dad get outside and walk more. All was going well but towards the end of their visit, Dad's medication was making him sick and his thyroid was acting up. They decided to head back home.

Along the way, they stopped by my stepsister's house to have a break and pick up their dog. After 12 hours of driving, Dad had a headache and wanted to lie down. As he walked to the bed, he kept dropping things.

When my stepmom went in to check on him, she knew something was wrong. They sat him up and he began vomiting blood. They rang the ambulance and upon arrival to the hospital, he was immediately booked in for brain surgery. Scans had shown blood pooling up in the brain area. They told my stepmom to prepare for the worst. Either he would die or he would have severe brain damage.

Again, I headed off to spend time with God. God took me to the story of Lazarus found in the book of John, Chapter 11. God spoke to me in a soft and gentle way saying,

> "Lazarus was my best friend. I knew that he had died. I knew he was with my Father in heaven. I also knew that I would be bringing him back to life. I knew all there was to know surrounding Lazarus yet when Mary and her friends and family came out to meet me in their sorrow, I wept. I wept at life and how far it had come from the original plan. I wept for Mary and her deep sorrow. I wept at the hurt and grief of the people I loved most. I wept at seeing my creation weep.
>
> Your father knows me like you do. You know where he will go when he leaves this earth. You know that he will be in a better place, an amazing, glorious place where he will never again experience pain or sorrow. He will be with me forever and that is a reason to rejoice. Yet it is okay to weep. For some things you will not comprehend until you are with me for eternity. Prepare to weep for your father is coming home."

I cried then. I cry now as I write this. I know where my father is and I know it is good, but I also know that it is okay to cry. I also cry at the mercy and love my Father in Heaven has for me. He cared enough to prepare me for what lay ahead.

As my family Skyped me again to say it was not looking good, I was given a supernatural peace. The next day they Skyped again to say that although his heart was beating and Dad was breathing with life support, the brain scan had shown that he was already gone. They would soon turn off the life support. I already knew before they said the words. Although they asked me to pray for a miracle, I knew I could not pray what was contrary to God's will.

I hung up. I sat at my kitchen counter in darkness and I began to thank my God that He had everything under control from the very beginning. There was nothing that was not in His plan. He had it all under control.

As I bowed my head in that moment, the presence of Jesus was there and I felt my father with Him! It was as if they were making one quick stop on the way home. There was so much happening in that moment, it is hard to put into words. I physically felt my father kiss me on the top of my head and I began to understand the blessing given in the Old Testament from a father to the first-born son. It was a time when things were put in order. Old regrets made right and all the words left unsaid were finally said. I felt comforted as the worldly troubles between my father and me vanished. I felt how proud he was of me and how, even though things didn't work out the way he wanted in this lifetime, all was set right now. I felt all the blessings that he wanted to bestow on me in his life were now passed on in a righteous manner before our Lord.

It was an amazing moment, but that was not the end of God's blessings in this matter. God also gave me a very personal symbol of his power and control.

My step-sister told me that when the ambulance came to pick up my dad, they asked her which hospital they would like my dad to be taken to. There are fourteen hospitals in their area. The main driver specified three particular hospitals he would recommend. My stepsister chose Riverside. Although she didn't know it, through this decision, God showed me again that everything was in His timing and in His plan.

Little did she know that Riverside was the very hospital where my father and I started our journey together.
You see, I was adopted by my parents. My dad loved to tell me the story of how he and my mother went to that hospital to adopt me. So it felt as if we had come a full circle. Everything surrounding my

father's death was in God's plan. Nothing escaped God's watchful eye; every "i" was dotted and "t" crossed. It was finished.

As soon as I thought God had closed that chapter and had finished speaking to me, He surprised me again with His compassion and love. While worshipping in church the following Sunday, the music transformed into a gateway of the divine. Along with our church singing, I could hear the angels singing and heaven bursting forth with song. Suddenly, I became aware of my father's presence in that place. Singing and dancing and rejoicing before our Lord and Savior. There were no dodgy knees holding him back or missed beats of a mechanical heart. He was whole in every way, confirming again and again, the goodness of my Lord.

Months later when both his birthday and Father's Day fell within the same week, I had a divine dream. I walked into a room and saw my father lying on the bed as he used to do when he was napping. He had his back to me and somehow I knew that he had been dead for three days. I went to lie down with him and put my arms around him as I did when I was a child. I thought to myself, 'I wish you were alive'. As soon as the thought was in my head, I heard a voice speak, 'Say in Jesus' name come back to life'. So I did and I felt Dad's chest rise and fall as he breathed. I heard the voice again, "Say in Jesus' name come back to life". So I said it again. This time he sat up and turned to face me. The smile on his face warmed my heart instantly as he whispered, "I miss you".

I replied, "I miss you too Daddy." I felt the roughness of his unshaven face, the warmth of his breath and even smelled his cologne. It was all just as I remembered as a kid.

He then said, "I have a surprise for you." He sat up and suddenly I could see his body. I knew that it looked like it did when he was in the air force, fit and healthy. He jumped up and his knees were solid.
I also noticed is that his face changed depending on the angle I looked at him. It reminded me of those bookmarks that change photos or make an animal look like it is running. When I looked to

the left, he was a young boy. When I looked to the right, he was as he looked just before his heart surgery. I could literally pick the way I wanted to see him.

I said, "I wish my step-mom and sister were here". And he replied, "They are". I turned around and there they sat, but they couldn't see Dad. They could sense his presence but their grief had blocked their sight. So I started to tell them everything Dad was telling me.

It was such a joyous time. Dad was eating something like bananas (apparently the kind you find in heaven) and he just couldn't get enough of them. He was telling me to tell the others how amazing they were, when suddenly I heard a voice say, "Enough" and all went instantly blank and it felt as if I fell back into my body again. I didn't realize how free I was until that feeling of coming back into my body, which just seemed confined, a bit sore and old.

Yes, it was a dream but it was so real at the same time. I remember it so clearly, even better than some of my "real" memories. I know that it may not make sense to others, but as I've said before, God knows exactly what I need and He has blessed me above all I could ever imagine.

A Stolen Purse

Faith is something that needs to be developed. You don't just wake up one day with faith. You have to experience struggles so that your faith may be developed. Christianity is not a religion, it is continuously moving. It is never stagnant and if you become complacent and stop going with the flow of the spirit then you are missing out on what being a follower of Christ really is.

I had just come home from a Ladies Retreat where faith was the focus and I was still contemplating all that I had learned when I was thrust right into my first lesson. It was the day after retreat when I took my four children into the shopping center to buy my daughter some clothes for summer. She had had another growth spurt recently so we had several t-shirts and shorts in our shopping cart.

I had my wallet buried in the bottom of a bag with all the clothes piled on top. As we were selecting some shorts, a woman came up and asked us where the children's section was. She said she always had a hard time finding clothes that fit her because she struggled with an eating disorder when she was young. Well, having been healed from an eating disorder myself, it touched my heart. So we spoke a bit more. When she left, I walked my daughter to the change rooms.

As we arrived, I had a sick and vile feeling come over me and I suddenly just knew I had been deceived. I looked in my bag and sure enough, my wallet had been stolen. She roped me in with her story so her friend could take what belonged to me.

After the first wave of shock rolled over me, I prayed. "Lord, you know that I did nothing wrong here. I showed love and compassion to another and have been robbed in the process. I pray your plans will succeed here. Please bring justice to me and this situation."

I went to the front service desk to report my stolen wallet and there was already another couple there reporting their bag as stolen. It also came out that bags behind the service desk were taken. This made me feel even worse; stress mounted and tears started to roll.

My youngest child was tugging on my pants, "I need to go to the toilet."

"Of all the times," I thought, as the toilet was halfway down the shopping center and I was trying to fill in information for the security guards. My daughter was still in the changing rooms trying on her clothes and I didn't want to leave the store.

As the pressure mounted, I didn't know what to do next so I just stood there upset and prayed for help. It was at that moment, I felt the presence of God. I looked up and saw a friend from church walk through the door.

"What happened?"

I simply said, "My wallet was stolen" and she just knew what to do. She took my youngest to the toilet. When she returned, we walked to get my daughter out of the change rooms. She had tried on all of her clothes and was waiting patiently for us. I asked the lady at the desk if she wanted me to return all the clothes to the shelves when my friend said she wanted to pay for the items.

"That is so kind of you," I replied. So I picked up a couple of items and left the rest in the cart.

"No, I want to pay for all of the items."

"I will pay you back when I get my wallet back or a new card. I promise."

"No, I have been blessed with extra money in my bank account today and now I know why. It is my gift to you."

I didn't know what made me cry more, the stolen wallet (with tears of grief) or this beautiful angel sent by God with such a gift of compassion (tears of gratitude). It was at that time I realized my church family truly is my family.

My husband then arrived to pick up the kids so that I could search the shopping center and the garbage bins for my wallet as I knew they often just grabbed the cash and would throw the rest away. I also wanted to search for the lady again as her face was etched in my mind. So I began to walk the entire shopping center, inside and out, searching. As I walked, I ran into so many people from church. It was as if God had called everyone to be there at just that time. I was so thankful. As I walked, I talked to God in my mind.

"God, I pray you will develop my faith. I don't have much faith but I know that I can muster up at least a seed's worth and your word says if I have as much faith as a mustard seed, I can move mountains. So I pray you will move mountains today."

Well, as I looked into the next shop, there was the lady! She was arguing with the clerk at the desk over a bag. I walked out and told the cleaning lady to call security. She did and as the two security guards walked up, I went in and approached the lady.

"Hi, do you remember me?"

"Um, no, I don't think so…"

"I was the one you discussed you eating disorder with, in Kmart, only 20 minutes ago"

"Oh"

"It was after I talked with you that I discovered my wallet went missing."

"That happened to my sister once."

"You don't think that the person who took my wallet would have dropped it accidentally into your cart do you?"

"Um, no, I don't think so."

"Then you don't mind if I have a look"

At this point, I looked generally in the bags nearest me, but she grabbed her purse and bag closer to her and became quite defensive to the security guards.

"I'm tired of you guys always following me and making accusations that I have stolen something."

Apparently, the security guards couldn't search her things lawfully without the police being present, so they just questioned her more. The security guard handling it told me that I should leave. They would contact me soon.

Well, it turned out they didn't have enough evidence to arrest her so they just let her go.

I went home exhausted. As I walked up to the door, I could see through the window my husband holding up his phone. I looked at him questioningly.

"I found your phone."

"What? How?"

"The new iPhones have tracking devices in them. It is at the Murdoch train station. It's been there for 30 minutes so I think they've thrown it in a bin."

I popped a banana in my mouth for dinner and called my eldest son. "Come on, we're going for a ride to the train station."

As we arrived, I checked in the bins but I didn't see any phones. I ran up to the security station and told them the situation. They said, "Unfortunately, we can't do anything without the police."

Frustrated, I used their phone to call the police. As I answered all their questions, my husband rang and said the phone was now on the train going to Perth. We decided I should come home until the phone stopped and then we could report it to the police.

We watched the phone go from one place to another all night. The next day it was still on the move from one shopping center to another. Finally, in the afternoon, the tracking system showed that my phone only had 12% of battery life left. I rang my husband.

"Mark, I am just so devastated. If we don't get this phone in the next 30 minutes, we're never going to see it again."

"I know. I'm on my way to the shopping center now."

"By yourself?"

"I'll get some security guards when I get there."

I hung up the phone and rang the police, trying to think of something to say that would motivate them to help us. I said to them, "We have been telling you where this phone has been all night and you have not done anything about it. Now my husband is on his way to get the phone himself and I'm worried about what will happen. He is upset and is determined to get it back. I just don't know what he will do."

I really did wonder what he would do but the police interpreted this as if my husband might do something violent. This motivated them into action, "I will check what police are in the area and will contact you soon."

I hung up and rang friends whom I knew would pray with me. Eight of us began praying for every aspect of the situation.

The police then rang and said, "Where is your husband?"

"At the shopping center."

"So are we, tell him we'll meet him in the west parking lot."

Well, the rest I have to tell you second-hand from my husband. As he pulled up to park, the police pulled up right behind him. They got out of the car and began to scan the parking lot as the tracker said the phone was somewhere in the area. Mark noticed a courier van parked with two guys just sitting in it, looking a bit suspicious. They walked towards the van and Mark rang the phone. They heard it ringing as the two tried to start the van to pull out. The police told them to turn off the engine as they questioned them.

"Where's your phone sir? I hear it ringing, where is it?"

They looked around a bit and finally, one of them pulled it out of his pocket. It still had my jellybean phone case on it! They showed it to Mark and as he nodded, identifying the phone, the police asked the two to step out of the van as they were being arrested for receiving stolen goods.

Days later the police station called me to come and identify from several photos, the woman who stole my bag. Having been a couple of days, I was nervous I would forget the details of what she looked like. Again, I asked God to help me recognize her. As I scanned the many photos of different women, her picture stood out to me clearly from all the rest. As I was leaving the station, they told me that I had picked the correct photo and now they could start court proceedings.

Although I had my phone back, I was almost sad when the week had ended. I felt like I was on a crime investigation show. But what amazed me was that, in the midst of such struggle, I had peace and joy knowing that God sees everything. Nothing is outside of His realm of power. He was able to guide me in every step. I don't have to worry about anyone or anything. I definitely can leave retribution up to Him, as His way of dealing with that is much better than I could ever do.

A daily devotion- 2 Kings 2

Many times God speaks to me as I daily come to Him to read the Bible and pray. I often journal what I learn and what God is teaching me. Here is an excerpt from my journal:

I was struggling at breakfast this morning deciding between reading my Bible verses or reading an interesting looking magazine that was sitting on my table. I don't recall saying it but I know somewhere within my mind I thought that the magazine looked a little more interesting than the Bible. I thought the Bible was a bit stagnant today, even briefly thinking my life was a bit that way too.

Not wanting to be disobedient, I flipped open the Bible and it literally fell to this chapter, 2 Kings 2. In this chapter, Elijah offered his apprentice Elisha the chance to stay home as he went on to Bethel.

> But Elisha said, "As sure as the Lord lives and as you live, I will not leave you." So they went down to Bethal.
>
> The company of prophets at Bethel came out to Elisha and asked, "Do you know that the Lord is going to take your master from you today?"
>
> "Yes I know," replied Elisha, "but do not speak of it."
> 2 Kings 2:2-3

Three times this scenario played out and all three times Elisha refused to leave his master's side to hang back and have fun with the other prophets. When they came to the Jordon River and Elijah struck it with his cloak so that the water parted, Elisha was the only prophet who walked across with Elijah to the other side. God brought this verse to my attention:

> *As they were walking along and talking together, suddenly a chariot of fire and horses of fire appeared and separated the two of them, and Elijah went up to heaven in a whirlwind.* 2 Kings 2:11

Elijah didn't die! He was taken to heaven in a chariot of fire! I then heard God speak into my mind. God asked me if I thought that would have been exciting or boring?

"Obviously exciting!", I answered.

God asked, "What do you think they walked and talked about before Elijah was taken in the chariot?"

I wondered about that conversation. "I have no idea", I replied.

"That's right and neither did the 500 other prophets who wanted to be there at that moment. That conversation will only be known between the two of them and me. Do you think that all the times Elisha followed and served Elijah would have been exciting?"

"It probably had its moments but most of the time it was probably just a slow and steady commitment to serving and spending time with him."

"Have you had some exciting moments with me?"

"Definitely."

"And do you think I have some exciting things yet to come? Is the commitment to never leave my side and serve me with everything you've got, worth it? Even when it's a bit mundane at times?"

"Yes."

God spoke and another lesson was learned.

God is always speaking, I've only spoken of a few ways He has spoken to me. Sometimes He speaks through His written word, the Bible. Other times, He communicates through different people or by speaking directly into my mind and heart. I've even had times when I've received answers from watching nature or listening to a song.

God has communicated with me in various ways but some of His most powerful lessons were learned through times of healing. God has revealed even more of who He is in the times that I have gone through physical struggles and relied on Him for healing, both physically and spiritually. In these times, I have not just heard from God, I have come to know Him.

Chapter 11
Healing
Does God still heal people?

O Lord my God, I called to you for help and you healed me.
Psalm 30:2

When Jesus began his ministry, He started by demonstrating His ability to heal people; and when Jesus healed people, well let's just say He didn't do things by halves! He healed hundreds and thousands of people.

> *Jesus went throughout Galilee, teaching in their synagogues, preaching the good news of the Kingdom, and healing every disease and sickness among the people. Matthew 4:23*

Why? The answer lies in the verses that follow:

> *News about him spread all over Syria... Large crowds from Galilee, the Decapolis, Jerusalem, Judea and the region across the Jordan followed him. Matthew 4:24-25*

Whole towns were coming to Him for healing. I mean who wouldn't? It got their attention then and it still has our attention today.

If a man in your suburb was teaching about God, would you go along? How about if he was healing people?

That certainly makes a difference, doesn't it? Healing gets people's attention. Jesus' ability to heal certainly got people's attention quickly. Jesus could, and still can heal people. He created humanity, so to heal someone physically is not too hard for Him. So why isn't everyone healthy and well? Let's go back a bit farther to the beginning of Jesus' ministry.

In Luke 4, Jesus went into the synagogue, as was His custom. He unrolled the scroll of Isaiah to read aloud and found the place where it was written:

> *The Spirit of the Lord is on me,*
> *Because he has anointed me*
> *To proclaim good news to the poor.*
> *He has sent me to proclaim freedom for the prisoners*
> *And recovery of sight for the blind*
> *To set the oppressed free,*
> *To proclaim the year of the Lord's favor.*
> *Luke 4:18-19 (Isaiah 61:1-2)*

This is the mission behind everything that Jesus does. Notice this statement says very little about physical healing and even the one reference to sight for the blind, speaks far more to me than just a physical healing. Jesus needed to get the crowds to come to Him so that He could teach them about the Kingdom of God.

Jesus doesn't just want your physical capsule to be fixed. He wants your spirit to be healed so that you will experience life to the fullest. Your physical body is only temporary but your spirit is eternal.

The spirit of man is much more important to God than the physical body. Physical healing is only temporary, as our bodies slowly degenerate every day until eventually, they cease to exist. Yes, Jesus healed people but it was only a matter of time until their body died just like everyone else. However, if Jesus healed the spirit then it had the potential to reside with Him forever.

When Jesus began His ministry, He was flooded with people wanting to be healed. But his healing of the masses was about to change. After spending some solitary time with His father at daybreak, He told them:

> *"I must proclaim the good news of the kingdom of God to the other towns also, because that is why I was sent." Luke 4:43*

He knew that if people understood the good news of the kingdom of God then their healing would eventually come. He tried to start with the religious leaders.

> *While Jesus was in one of the towns, a man came along who was covered with leprosy. When he saw Jesus, he fell with his face to the ground and begged him,*
>
> *"Lord, if you are willing, you can make me clean."*
>
> *Jesus reached out his hand and touched the man.*
>
> *"I am willing," he said. "Be clean!" And immediately the leprosy left him.*
>
> *Then Jesus ordered him, "Don't tell anyone, but go, show yourself to the priest and offer the sacrifices that Moses commanded for your cleansing, as a testimony to them." Luke 5: 12-14*

Jesus heals the man with leprosy but then tells him to go show himself to the priest and offer the sacrifices that Moses commanded for cleansing, "as a testimony to them." Who is this testimony for?

He wants this healing to be a testimony to those in the synagogue, the place where people come to learn about God. Jesus wants the leaders and those who are religious, those who have diligently studied the word and sought God all of their lives, to understand what is happening right in the midst of them.

Jesus offered a way to eternal life! To be completely healed from death itself. He wanted religious leaders to get on board to share the good news. He desired the religious leaders to be the first to learn about this new life so that they could offer healing to others themselves. Instead, they were filled with jealousy and judgment.

Jesus attempted to reach out to the religious leaders again when He healed a paralyzed man lowered from the rooftop by his friends because the crowds were too dense.

> *When Jesus saw their faith, he said, "Friend, your sins are forgiven."*
>
> *The Pharisees and the teachers of the law began thinking to themselves, "Who is this fellow who speaks blasphemy? Who can forgive sins but God alone?"*
>
> *Jesus knew what they were thinking and asked, "Why are you thinking these things in your hearts?*

(Proof alone that God looks at the heart of man, not the outward appearance)

> *Which is easier: to say, 'Your sins are forgiven,' or to say, 'Get up and walk'? But I want you to know that the Son of Man has authority on earth to forgive sins." So he said to the paralyzed man, "I tell you, get up, and take your mat and go home."*

> *Immediately he stood up in front of them, took what he had been lying on and went home praising God.   Luke 5:17-25*

He uses this healing as a symbol of the much greater thing that Jesus is able to do. Jesus is able to forgive your sins, give your soul freedom and your heart healing.

As you read on in Luke 6, you begin to see that it is people's mindsets that need healing more than any physical ailment. The Pharisees and teachers of the law were following Jesus but for all the wrong reasons.

> *The Pharisees and the teachers of the law were looking for a reason to accuse Jesus, so they watched him closely to see if He would heal on the Sabbath. Luke 6:7*

The Pharisees spent endless hours arguing over the laws of the Sabbath (a day designated for rest). They would argue over whether a man could or could not carry a lamp from one point to another on the Sabbath or whether a tailor committed a sin if he went out with a needle in his robe. If a woman wore a brooch or if a man had false teeth; if someone had an artificial limb or even lifted a child, that person might be accused of breaking the Sabbath. "Their religion was a legalism of petty rules and regulations."[4]

Again Jesus uses healing to teach the more divine truths of God.

> *But Jesus knew what they were thinking and said to the man with the shriveled hand, "Get up and stand in front of everyone."*
> *...I ask you, which is lawful on the Sabbath: to do good or to do evil, to save life or to destroy it?"*

---

[4] bible.org/seriespage/Sabbath-controversy-gospels

> *He looked around at them all, and then said to the man, "Stretch out your hand." He did so, and his hand was completely restored.*
> Luke 6:9

The same incident happens again in another synagogue. There was a woman that had been crippled for eighteen years, bent over and couldn't stand up. When the woman came to Jesus to be healed, the synagogue ruler went so far as to say

> *"There are six days for work. So come and be healed on those days, not on the Sabbath."* Luke 13:14

Can you imagine getting in trouble from the church priests for wanting to be healed? Jesus was not impressed, to say the least:

> *"You hypocrites! Doesn't each of you on the Sabbath untie your ox or donkey from the stall and lead it out to give it water? Then should not this woman, a daughter of Abraham, whom Satan has kept bound for eighteen long years, be set free on the Sabbath day from what bound her?"* Luke 13:10-17

These religious leaders were the people that were supposed to be representing God, yet they didn't even know Him! Jesus was angered by how petty people could be in their religious traditions back then.

Yet, I would challenge us to look carefully at ourselves today. What sort of rules are we implementing in our standards to love others? Are we not just as guilty to judge others based on petty things; outer appearance, maybe a person has tattoos, smokes or wears clothes we don't like? We may even judge on inner appearance. They have different beliefs than me or a lifestyle I don't approve of. Notice Jesus did not heal people on the basis that they were perfect Christians; quite the contrary. Jesus said;

> *It is not the healthy who need a doctor, but the sick. I have not come to call the righteous, but sinners. Mark 2:17*

Jesus healed people because He wanted to free them, physically and spiritually. He wanted to show the religious leaders how to love others as God does. He wanted them to start a revolution in the way people think and act towards each other.

Do you realize that when Jesus came to earth, He perfectly fulfilled more than three hundred prophecies recorded in the Old Testament on how to recognize the Savior when He arrives? The very people who had the scrolls that contained the written word, studied and taught from those scrolls, the ones who should have understood God more than anyone, didn't recognize Jesus as the Son of God. How frustrating to have a church that didn't even recognize God when He was right in the midst of them!

Do we dare think we are any better at recognizing Him today? And yes, you will still see evidence of Jesus everywhere if you look carefully enough. Do we recognize God in the midst of our lives today? Have you bothered to take the time to look for God or do you just assume you know enough about God and live the way that you want? As a church body, are we praying and seeking God with everything we have so that we may represent Him in an honoring and pleasing way?

To those who did recognize Jesus, their faith alone brought their healing.

> *When Jesus had entered Capernaum, a centurion came to him, asking for help. 'Lord,' he said, 'my servant lies at home paralyzed and in terrible suffering.'*
> *Jesus said to him, 'I will go and heal him.'*
> *The centurion replied, 'Lord, I do not deserve to have you come under my roof. But just say the word, and my servant will be*

> *healed. For I myself am a man under authority, with soldiers under me. I tell this one, 'Go,' and he goes; and that one, 'Come,' and he comes. I say to my servant, 'Do this,' and he does it.'*
>
> *When Jesus heard this, he was astonished and said to those following him, 'I tell you the truth, I have not found anyone in Israel with such great faith...'*
>
> *Then Jesus said to the centurion, 'Go! It will be done just as you believed it would.'*
>
> *And his servant was healed at that very hour.*
>
> *Matthew 8:5-13 (Also found in Luke 7:1-10)*

The faith this man held truly impressed Jesus. Stop. Imagine for a moment, impressing the Son of God. Jesus had not seen such great faith displayed in all of Israel! There is no teaching here because this man already gets it. He knows who Jesus is and what He is capable to do as the one sent by God. He understands as one commander to another how things work. A centurion was a commander in the Ancient Roman army and Jesus is the commander of the armies of heaven. (Rev. 19:11-21, 2 Tim. 2:3-4, Joshua 5:15)

Later in Luke 8:40, a synagogue leader came to Jesus and fell at His feet. He pleaded with Jesus to come to his house because his only daughter, a girl of about twelve, was dying. I can just imagine how moved Jesus was to have a synagogue leader come to him. Finally, the good news was beginning to sink in!

Jesus is on his way to the house of the synagogue leader and in the midst of a large crowd another act of faith brings about instantaneous healing.

> *As Jesus was on his way, the crowds almost crushed him. And a woman was there who had been subject to bleeding for twelve years, but no one could heal her. She came up behind him and*

touched the edge of his cloak, and immediately her bleeding stopped.

Who touched me?' Jesus asked.

When they all denied it, Peter said, 'Master, the people are crowding and pressing against you.'

But Jesus said, 'Someone touched me; I know that power has gone out from me.'

Then the woman, seeing that she could not go unnoticed, came trembling and fell at his feet. In the presence of all the people, she told why she had touched him and how she had been instantly healed. Then he said to her, 'Daughter, your faith has healed you. Go in peace.' Luke 8:42-48

A bleeding woman, who would be considered ceremonially unclean to the society at that time, was outcast because of her very embarrassing medical problem. So she pushed through a large crowd, took a leap of faith, and just simply touched the cloak of Jesus believing it would heal her. Jesus was so moved by her faith, He had to turn and find her in the midst of a very large crowd.

"Take heart, daughter," He said, "your **faith** has healed you." The woman was healed because of her faith.

This story in particular really impacted the disciples as it is told in three separate accounts: Mark 5:21-43, Matthew 9:18-26, Luke 8:40-56.

It proves that God's love is not based on who you are. It's based on who He is. It doesn't matter who you are or what your background is, Jesus loves you.

Unfortunately, what people don't understand is that instant physical healing has the potential to be quite detrimental to the soul, in that once a person is healed of their physical ailment it becomes quite easy to just go on with life and forget about continuing a relationship with God. The latter being far more important than anything else.

> *As He (Jesus) was going into a village, ten men who had leprosy met him. They stood at a distance and called out in a loud voice, "Jesus, Master, have pity on us!" When he saw them, he said, "Go, show yourselves to the priests." And as they went they were cleansed.*
>
> *One of them, when he saw he was healed, came back, praising God in a loud voice. He threw himself at Jesus' feet and thanked him- and he was a Samaritan.* Luke 17:11-19

Only one out of ten came back to thank God. And he was a Samaritan, despised by the Jews for not being holy enough.

How ungrateful we are for the many good things we receive every day. When is the last time you thanked God for the blessings in your life?

When you are physically ill do you question God? Do you search with your whole being, mind and soul, as to why you are going through this and what will happen next? It is an excellent place for your heart to be, searching. At least when you are searching, you have an understanding that you are missing something. Even as a Christian, you are more dependent on God when you need healing and in a place where you can learn lessons that He wants to teach you.

Jesus taught many valuable lessons from His healings:

> *As he went along, he saw a man blind from birth. His disciples asked him, "Rabbi, who sinned, this man or his parents, that he was born blind?"*
>
> *"Neither this man nor his parents sinned, " said Jesus, "but this happened so that the work of God might be displayed in his life." John 9:1-3*

Generally, people want a nice neat and packaged answer for illness, disabilities or suffering. We even love to label and stick something or someone in a category so it can fit nicely in our perception of our world. When it doesn't happen, we're not quite sure what to do. Why? Because we are not in control. God is not performing to our expectations or demands. We blame Him for things that we conveniently label as a disability when we never have stopped to ask Him what He might call it. In our little minds, we put standards in place for a "Successful Life" and when people don't live up to our standards, we feel sorry for them. Have you ever thought it might be the other way around?

You might be surprised to know that many people in third world nations are praying for those in the wealthy west because so many people are depressed, anxious, and have lost their way. They pray for those in churches to go beyond just Christmas and Easter visits to a real relationship with God.
Often those we label disabled are more whole than we will ever understand. The people we label 'disabled', often have a clearer understanding of what is important in life than many people labeled 'normal'. The blind can see so much more than we ever will.

Paul had a physical ailment that plagued him throughout his ministry. He prayed to God and learned to see his pain in a different way. Here is what he wrote in his letter to the Corinthians:

> *To keep me from becoming conceited because of these surpassingly great revelations, there was given me a thorn in my flesh, a messenger of Satan, to torment me. Three times I pleaded with the Lord to take it away from me. But he said to me, "My grace is sufficient for you, for my power is made perfect in weakness."*
>
> *Therefore I will boast all the more gladly about my weaknesses so that Christ's power may rest on me. That is why, for Christ's sake, I delight in weaknesses, in insults, in hardships, in persecutions, in difficulties. For when I am weak then I am strong.*
> *2 Corinthians 12:7-10*

Take time to bring your health problems to God. Ask God to open your spiritual eyes to what is really happening in your body. Are there spiritual lessons that God wants to teach you. Is there another way to view this? Is your health issue a problem or a blessing in disguise? Would healing bring you closer to God or would you just 'get on with life' and forget about Him? How can you be close to God now in the midst of your suffering?

Chapter 12
A journey in healing
How does God heal people?

Heal me, O Lord, and I will be healed; save me and I will be saved, for you are the one I praise."
Jeremiah 17:14

Several years ago, I woke up one morning to what felt like lightning pulsating back and forth throughout my body. I couldn't move and struggled just to breathe. I have never felt pain so intense and for so long. My husband called an ambulance and the only thing I remember is how grateful I was that someone discovered pain-relief medication in a little green tube you breathe into during your ambulance ride.

I could barely move for 4 days and then with crutches was able to begin a slow and painful journey back to walking again. Although you may never have experienced sciatica, I think you may relate to some of my experiences.

I felt alone because no one else was experiencing my pain. I felt guilty that other people, mainly my husband and children, had to do everything in my place. I felt upset at the timing of this, not that there ever is a good time to experience pain and suffering. I felt weak and discouraged. I spent way too much time with all the questions in my head: Will I ever feel better or am I stuck with this for life? What if the intense pain comes back? I even spent a good amount of time in the throws of depression, especially in the early days of such excruciating pain, thinking it would be a good time for God to just take me home.

After the initial onslaught of pain, when I started to get out of the house and see people again, I experienced a different kind of pain. Whether it was real or perceived, I felt people looked at me differently. I realized many were uncomfortable around me. Others filled the awkward silence with well-intentioned advice. I experienced a very unnerving feeling when someone said, "Oh, you poor thing" and gave me a pat on the back and a promise to pray as they walked on, not even looking at me.

Another person told me that they had sciatica before but took aspirin and was better the next day. Surprisingly, I didn't find that encouraging.

Yet as I began to pray to God, He began to use this experience to teach me some very insightful spiritual lessons. Lessons that honestly I wouldn't learn unless I was in this particular situation. God allowed me to feel the pain of other people's responses because as sad as I am to admit this, I was one of those who responded pretty much the same way. I'm horrified at how quickly I have been to dismiss other people's pain in the past. I pray I will be more careful from now on with the words I say when people come to me with their suffering.

I have learned that each person feels things differently. Just because I've gone through and survived something that looks vaguely similar to what they are going through does not mean that I understand or that I am any better. I do not need to have answers nor do I need to be speaking just to fill in the silence. I simply need to respond with love and compassion.

For me, the most comfort came from people who have truly experienced pain, no matter what kind of pain it was. They understood in ways that others who had not gone through a painful experience could ever understand. Their offers to pray for me, to drive me to places, just showing up to clean my house, or making themselves available if I needed them have meant so much. Just knowing someone was praying for me, helped me through so many painful nights when I felt I couldn't go on any further.

Another thing I have learned is that the world truly can go on without me. I have seen family and friends fill in and perform my daily tasks better and more efficiently. This has been a good serve of humble pie for me but it has taught me that I really do have the time to prioritize what God calls me to do. The people around me will adjust just fine.

Along with learning to prioritize, I also learned to slow down. I have missed out on opportunities and have rushed through my life all in the excuse of being too busy. My conversations have been compromised to a couple of sentences and I have missed the joy of simply stopping and taking in the scenery around me; to literally smell the roses, enjoy my garden or view the beautiful sunsets. I know this will always be something I need to be mindful of because as my pain improves I can feel "busy" ness trying to creep its way back into my life every day, and, if left unattended to, it will fight to control my life again.

I was so blessed during this time to talk and share with our beautiful older generation and also with people who have various disabilities. As I hobbled on crutches and worked my way around shopping centers, I had nods of understanding and smiles sent my way from those in similar situations. I had never had this happen before, or had I simply been in too much of a hurry to notice? I will never know but it seemed my crutches were a key into many newfound friendships.

Even during my short stay in the hospital, I was surprised at how many friendships were formed with the most amazing people from nursing staff, who are heroes in my opinion, to other patients who encouraged me. I think I liked it so much because conversations were real and weren't spent fluffing about on frivolities. Isn't it a beautiful thing that in the midst of illness and physical suffering it opens up doors to knowing people we may have never had the chance to meet before?
I was very blessed and had several people from church make meals for my family. Some of the people I didn't even know, so imagine how surprised I was! But one day I got an even bigger

surprise. One beautiful lady made me some dishes that were gluten and dairy-free because she knew that is what my son and I could eat. I was blown away.

I don't want you to perceive this in the wrong way. I am truly thankful and feel immensely blessed by all who took the time to help our family. I am only writing this to take it to another level, at least for me. I have learned that as a Christian who lives in a face-paced world, I rarely slow down to notice other peoples' specific needs. I have spent a lot of time on what I perceived would be helpful to someone else and then would drop it at the door and leave. But now that I have experienced how nice it feels to have someone go the "extra mile" to find out what I enjoyed eating, I will endeavor to do the same for someone else next time.

I learned it is important to call out for help in times of need. One of my closest friends was there to help every step of the way. I was doubly blessed that she was not working at the time so she had the time to encourage me and help me in so many ways. I know she was searching hard for a job at the time and most likely felt suffering in this but had she found a job, I know I would not have recovered at the rate I did and there would be nothing left of my husband. So I am so very thankful for her misfortune at the time. I bring this up because you may never understand what a blessing you can be in what you deem as a time of suffering.

I also called on the elders and the people of the church to pray for me as it is written:

> *Is anyone of you sick? He should call the elders of the church to pray over him and anoint him with oil in the name of the Lord. And the prayer offered in faith will make the sick person well; the Lord will raise him up. If he has sinned, he will be forgiven. Therefore confess your sins to each other and pray for each other so that you may be healed. The prayer of a righteous man is powerful and effective. James 5:14-15*

Often people offer to help but we don't call them, usually due to our pride issues. This not only makes you feel isolated but also stops someone else from receiving the blessing of helping you. A friend gave me some good advice, "Stop being so snobby and let someone help you! You will make their day!"

Finally, it was in the midst of my darkest moments that I learned about the power of worship. This is a divine spiritual area that goes beyond words but is vital to healing and communing with God. Worship looks different for every person. It's about getting lost in the wonder of God.

Although I didn't feel like it, when I was at my lowest points physically or mentally, I would put on some Christian music and begin singing to God and worshipping Him. Sometimes I would simply begin to thank God for the many blessings in my life. There were times I would lay in my bed watching the leaves on the tree outside of my window. As they swayed and the light patterns changed on my bedroom wall, I thought about how all of creation worships God in its own way. It was a very intimate time with God and healing took place.

It is important to worship God. Whether you tell Him or write to Him in prayer, sing to Him in a song, show it by bowing down on bended knees, or just being still in reverence while experiencing nature, whatever it looks like, as you glorify God, He will tend to your spirit and you will be changed.

When I stop to think about it, so much was learned from this experience that I'm almost glad I've been through it. I can certainly say that the experience wasn't a waste of time. Hindsight often makes things easier to comprehend.

So, do I think that God caused this? No. Most of it was consequential to some bad decisions I've made rushing around and not prioritizing God, trying to fix things myself rather than asking God or others for help, pushing myself to be some sort of supermom and entering the deadly arena of comparison. I was juggling way too much physically and mentally. Satan only needed to add fuel to an already lit flame and whoosh, the fire became out of control. Yet, I knew that God knew what was coming and decided that it would be a great time for me to learn some new lessons about myself and my God.

Awhile back I saw a British television show where people would bring their most embarrassing health issues, things they've been ashamed of for years, to share with doctors in front of thousands of television viewers. I can't say I understand the reasoning in that, but one thing I admired about the show is that the doctors never flinched. They looked at the most disgusting health problems and they treated the person with respect. They never laughed or mocked but simply offered advice that brought about healing.

God is not interested in anything but getting you better. Nothing will shock Him or cause Him to turn away in disgust. He loves you!!! You can bring anything to Him and He will help you. Just as medicine and surgery are not things of pleasure, sometimes they are a necessary means to a healthy ending and God's ways are the same. They may not always be fun but He will only ask you to do what is necessary to bring about healing.

There are many things that God knows about me that are very intimate; mistakes I've made and dark places I've been. These are journeys that I now understand we have gone through together. Deep down I didn't want God to see some of the awful things I did. The exposure of that sin to His Holiness was something I tried to justify my way out of. Now that I have changed and healed, I thank Him that He went through it with me. He went to those embarrassing places and helped me to get out, to be healed and to be free.

Often if our spiritual problems are left unattended they turn into physical problems. It is well documented that stress can cause all sorts of physical problems from migraines to back problems to just about anything you can name! Stress can cause a lot of physical damage. If stress can do that, imagine what physical ailments could happen if you harbored bitterness, grudges, anger, resentment, guilt and shame. These are the problems God wants to treat. As we begin to heal in our spiritual bodies, I believe that healing works its way out to our physical situations.

What are your symptoms telling you? Is there a bigger problem at the root of your symptoms? Would you be willing to let Jesus in to deal with the cause of the problem? God is more concerned about the state of your heart than He is about your physical and temporary body.

> '...The Lord does not look at the things people look at. People look at the outward appearance, but the Lord looks at the heart.'
>
> 1 Samuel 16:7

How is your heart? Are you at peace in your life? Don't let guilt or shame stop you from seeking God. Guilt and shame are from the devil: God works differently. He will convict your spirit to get you to change. He has already forgiven you for anything and everything. He wants you to be free of guilt and shame.

Healing is very personal and there are no simplistic answers. God wants to journey with you through your sickness. Only He alone understands what is necessary for your healing and He wants you to come to Him. Could you begin to believe in the power of Jesus, like the centurion and the woman with the bleeding issue?

Before I close this chapter, I want to share with you some of the Bible verses that have helped me to understand healing and have helped to bring about healing in my life. Notice that in all of them there is a close connection between physical health and spiritual health. Many of them have some important instructions included to bring about healing. If you would like to experience healing in some way in your life, take time to read and think about what each verse is saying. I pray God will open the eyes of your heart that you may understand what He is saying to you.

Blessed is he who has regard for the weak; the Lord delivers him in times of trouble. The Lord will protect him and preserve his life; he will bless him in the land and not surrender him to the desire of his foes. The Lord will sustain him on his sickbed and restore him from his bed of illness. I said, "O Lord, have mercy on me; heal me, for I have sinned against you.   Psalm 41:1-4

The righteous cry out, and the Lord hears them; he delivers them from all their troubles. The Lord is close to the brokenhearted and saves those who are crushed in Spirit.   Psalm 34:17-18

Praise the Lord, O my soul; all my inmost being, praise his holy name. Praise the Lord, O my soul, and forget not all his benefits; who forgives all your sins and heals all your diseases, who redeems your life from the pit and crowns you with love and compassion, who satisfies your desires with good things so that your youth is renewed like the eagle's.   Psalm 103:1-5

He sent forth His word and healed them; he rescued them from the grave. Let them give thanks to the Lord for his unfailing love and his wonderful deeds for men. Let them sacrifice thank offerings and tell of his works with songs of joy. Psalm 107:20-22

I will heal my people and will let them enjoy abundant peace and security.   Jeremiah 33:6b

Then they cried to the Lord in their trouble, and he saved them from their distress. He sent forth his word and healed them; he rescued them from the grave.   Psalm 107: 19-21

Isaiah 58: 1-14 is a long passage but well worthy of study and meditation to understand healing[5]:

'Shout it aloud, do not hold back.
Raise your voice like a trumpet.
Declare to my people their rebellion
and to the descendants of Jacob their sins.
For day after day they seek me out;
they seem eager to know my ways,
as if they were a nation that does what is right
and has not forsaken the commands of its God.
They ask me for just decisions
and seem eager for God to come near them.
'Why have we fasted,' they say,
'and you have not seen it?
Why have we humbled ourselves,
and you have not noticed?'
Yet on the day of your fasting, you do as you please
and exploit all your workers.
Your fasting ends in quarreling and strife,

and in striking each other with wicked fists.
You cannot fast as you do today
and expect your voice to be heard on high.
Is this the kind of fast I have chosen,

---

[5] Emphasis is mine.

only a day for people to humble themselves?
Is it only for bowing one's head like a reed
and for lying in sackcloth and ashes?
Is that what you call a fast,
a day acceptable to the Lord?
Is not this the kind of fasting I have chosen:
to loose the chains of injustice
and untie the cords of the yoke,
to set the oppressed free
and break every yoke?
Is it not to share your food with the hungry
and to provide the poor wanderer with shelter-
when you see the naked, to clothe them,
and not to turn away from your own flesh and blood.
Then your light will break forth like the dawn,
and your <u>healing</u> will quickly appear;
then your righteousness will go before you,
and the glory of the Lord will be your rear guard.
Then you will call, and the Lord will answer;
you will cry for help, and he will say: Here am I.
If you do away with the yoke of oppression,
    with the pointing finger and malicious talk,
and if you spend yourselves in behalf of the hungry
    and satisfy the needs of the oppressed,
then your light will rise in the darkness,
    and your night will become like the noonday.
The Lord will guide you always;

> he will <u>satisfy your needs</u> in a sun-scorched land
> and <u>will strengthen your frame</u>.
> You will be like a well-watered garden,
> like a spring whose waters never fail.
> Your people will rebuild the ancient ruins
> and will raise up the age-old foundations;
> you will be called Repairer of Broken Walls,
> Restorer of Streets with Dwellings.
> If you keep your feet from breaking the Sabbath
> and from doing as you please on my holy day,
> if you call the Sabbath a delight
> and the Lord's holy day honorable,
> and if you honor it by not going your own way
> and not doing as you please or speaking idle words,
> then you will <u>find your joy</u> in the Lord,
> and I will cause you to ride in triumph on the heights of the land
> and to feast on the inheritance of your father Jacob.'
> For the mouth of the Lord has spoken.

It seems I learn something new every time I experience a physical ailment. I can't say that I'm happy going through illness and injury but I am truly grateful God uses these experiences because they have truly helped to make me into a better person.

You may have an illness of some sort as you are reading this. I want to pray for you right now:

Lord, I pray that you will reveal yourself at this time. Help us to open our hearts and our minds that you may teach us the spiritual lessons we need to learn. Help us to learn to be a better person. As our hearts heal, I pray that healing will work its way out into our physical beings. Lord, we don't understand why we are going through this and that is okay because we don't need to but if it is your will, please show us what you are trying to teach us so that we may work with you and not against you. Help us to place our faith in you and your love for us. May we have compassion for others as you have compassion for us. Use this experience to strengthen our faith in you. **Amen.**

> *My son, pay attention to what I say; listen closely to my words. Do not let them out of your sight, keep them within your heart; for they are life to those who find them and health to a man's whole body. Above all else, guard your heart, for it is the wellspring of life. Proverbs 4:20-23*

I am a firm believer that healing is a lifestyle and that God works from the inside out. Yes, He can instantly heal you as we have seen in the passages above but if He has your attention with your current situation, He can do so much more than physically heal you. He wants to use everything to strengthen your faith. For when you have faith, miracles happen.

Yet there is an obstacle that stands in the way of healing. That obstacle is sin. Jesus overcame this obstacle by taking the consequences of our sin to the cross and overcoming sin altogether. Yet when we refuse to admit our sin or repent of it, it becomes a stumbling block in our lives. We have to face our sin and deal with it. That is part of maturing or growing up in the Christian faith.

Chapter 13
Grow up!
Why do Christians seem like such hypocrites?

...Until we all reach unity in the faith and in the knowledge of the Son of God and become mature...
Ephesians 4:13

When you accept Jesus Christ as the Lord of your life and allow Him on the throne of the control room in your life, you start your life again, with a fresh, clean slate. You may have heard the expression, 'born again'. This is not because you have physically been born again, but because you have begun a new life with God. You've in essence, hit the 'delete' button of the old life and have started a fresh page. This expression, 'born again' comes from the following passage of the Bible:

> Now there was a man of the Pharisees named Nicodemus, a ruler of the Jews. This man came to Jesus by night and said to him, "Rabbi, we know that you are a teacher come from God, for no one can do these signs that you do unless God is with him." Jesus answered him, "Truly, truly, I say to you, unless one is born again he cannot see the kingdom of God."
>
> Nicodemus said to him, "How can a man be born when he is old? Can he enter a second time into his mother's womb and be born?"
>
> Jesus answered, "Truly, truly, I say to you, unless one is born of water and the Spirit, he cannot enter the kingdom of God. That

> *which is born of the flesh is flesh, and that which is born of the Spirit is spirit." John 3:1-6*

God wants to teach us new ways of thinking, speaking, acting and living. He doesn't want us to live as everyone else does. He wants to teach us so many amazing, beautiful things; things that we just can't comprehend without Him imparting it within us: like the complete freedom that comes with obedience, the peace that only comes in suffering and love beyond what we could ever imagine.

He wants us to grow and develop our faith. This spiritual journey is very similar to the way a child grows, learns and matures. We learn a little bit at a time. We stumble and make mistakes and we learn how to get back up again. The more we seek after God, the more God reveals Himself.

> *Ask and it will be given to you; seek and you will find; knock and the door will be opened to you. For everyone who asks receives; he who seeks finds; and to him who knocks, the door will be opened- Matthew 7:7-8*

The more time we spend with God, we begin to think deeper and become more intimate with his thoughts and understanding. We begin to grow in our spiritual life. We wrestle with various lessons in life and grow from them. With maturity comes contentment and satisfaction. As we begin to understand life and our purpose in it, peace begins to settle in our hearts.

That's how a Christian's walk is meant to be. However, not all of us mature the way we are meant to. Some of us remain stuck at the starting block of Christianity either too afraid or too stubborn to move forward. Paul addresses Christians with this problem:

> *Brothers and sisters, I could not address you as people who live by the Spirit but as people who are still worldly – mere infants in*

> *Christ. I gave you milk, not solid food, for you were not ready for it. Indeed, you are still not ready. You are still worldly. For since there is jealousy and quarreling among you, are you not worldly: Are you not acting like mere humans?* 1 Corinthians 3:1-3

Let's get one thing straight. God loves you. He will always love you whether you are blossoming in righteousness or being a spoilt brat. He will not, however, love the sin in your life and He will use the circumstances and consequences you bring into your life to get rid of that sin. He loves you, even if it takes tough-love to bring you to where you are meant to be in life. Sometimes you need a push off the starting block to put your faith in motion.

We won't appreciate this kind of love until we mature, just like children don't appreciate the love and discipline of their parents until they get older and mature. It's the same with the children of God. We just don't comprehend how much God loves us. Although His discipline is sometimes hard to understand, we need to know that He does what He does to bring us closer to Him. God wants us to have something special in our relationship with Him. Sadly this is something that many people will never really understand.

God uses many things to mature us. We've already discussed how trials and struggles make us stronger and more mature in our Christian faith but God also uses relationships to grow us in our faith.

Why am I going on about relationships?

God matures us spiritually through the concepts learned from relationships. He works within us individually, in our relationship with Him and through the relationships we have with those He created around us. If you want to mature in Christ, you cannot avoid relationship issues. You either remain immature or you work through them, develop and grow wiser.

Our relationship with God is a complexity in itself. He is not just God but through the various names of God, we come to understand that He has a relationship with us as a King, a Father, a friend, a teacher and a soulmate. He alone can fulfill every relationship we need in our lives. If any of those relationships have been missing in our lives, He is able to fill the void.

He understands the damage that we as humans tend to do to each other and it grieves His heart that His creation would behave like this but He understands sin in a way we never will. When we come to God in a relationship, He wants to heal those areas that have been damaged or destroyed by others.

I have never met a person yet that has not been hurt or damaged by someone through verbal or physical abuse, intentional or unintentional harm or simply lack of presence when needed. God heals the gaps or damage so well because He knows how to be all things to us, whatever our need. He helps us to understand and mature in our relationship with Him by our relationships with others. And it's usually in the more difficult relationships that we mature.

I'm sure you won't have to look far to find that difficult relationship. You can't escape it. It's either already in your family, amongst your friends or in the church you attend. If you don't have any then I would say that you have been shying away from any relationships beyond the acquaintance level.

I used to run away from my difficult relationships and honestly, that is still my first gut reaction. I hate conflict! Life is just so much nicer without it. Not only do I not want to be hurt but I don't want to hurt others either, so I rationalize in my mind that it's just better to ignore it and go our separate ways. But with God, I have found the courage to face some of these difficult relationships and I have matured in my faith and in the way I deal with people around me.

Many people who come to church have been "burnt" in the past by others, and unfortunately, most were hurt by other Christians. This is a very sad but common problem we are facing today. Yet instead of focusing on past hurt, Jesus wants to bring freedom so we can get up again and move forward. If you have been hurt, on behalf of the church I want to say to you, "I'm sorry."

Stop.

I want you to listen to me, although I'm writing, I want you to hear me saying this.

I am so sorry for what you have been through. I know that God did not want things to end the way they did.

> I am sorry for the hurtful words left stinging in your heart.
>
> I am sorry for the way it made you feel.
>
> I'm sorry that untruthful things were implied about your character.
>
> I'm sorry that it made you feel resentful against the church and against God.

I ask now for your forgiveness of the church, the body of Christ. I can't even promise you that it won't happen again. Chances are it will. But I know that if you give God a chance and don't run away but seek His way, He will help you to work through the seemingly impossible and you will learn so many aspects of God and who He is.

The thing is, I know what it is like to be hurt. It's deep and shakes you in ways you've never imagined. I also know what it's like to get caught up in that hurt and wallow in it for months and into years. Holding onto the hurt only hurts us. Holding onto hurt only leads to bitterness which eventually develops into a pride issue. I can guarantee that you stewing over what someone has done to you is not bothering them. And if you are purposely bothering them by bringing it up every time you see them, then you are the one who is lacking in maturity. Ouch!

Okay, here comes the hard part, I am going to do my best to speak the truth in love so that you may mature and be closer to God. If you are unable to hear the ugly truth about yourself you will never be able to grasp the intimacy you so long to have with God.

Many of us are quick to see the problems in others but forget that we do a lot of hurt and damage ourselves.

What I'm trying to get at is that many people whine and complain about God saying that God is unjust, uncaring, or not even there, when they don't want to give Him a chance to show that they might be wrong.

Ok, here are the hard truths that most people probably tippy-toe around and don't want to tell you because you are that person with a stinky attitude. I don't know you so I'm going to write freely the things that most people wish they could say to you.

You are NOT always right. Truth be known, you're rarely right.

The people around you make mistakes. Yes, even the so-called "Christians".

A Christian is a follower of Jesus Christ. They are **NOT** Jesus Christ.

Christians have just as many sins as everyone else. The church is full of sinners! The only difference is that Christians are on a journey with God to change.

We as Christians cannot save you from the manure going on in your life and all the sin that you are entangled in but we can point you in the right direction to someone who can. So please do not expect the church to fix all of your problems.
The world does not revolve around you and your opinions.

God is bigger than you can ever imagine, wiser than you could ever dream and knows you better than you know yourself.

God will not do what YOU want Him to do. He will do what is best for you.

God does not have to explain Himself to you, although if you curb your stinky attitude for just a moment, you might find He often will.

Finally, who do you think you are? What makes you think God, creator of the universe, stars, oceans, people, heavens and beyond is answerable to you? Before you begin to question God, the Bible or Christians, think about this. Do you really want to know the answers or are you just asking the questions to "prove" that you are right?

There, I hope you're still with me. I know that may not have been pleasant, but these are truths we all have to learn, including me. And if you just finished reading that section thinking to yourself "Finally someone is saying what everyone around me needs to hear", go back and read it again because I'm not talking to the people around you, I'm talking to you. These hard truths are also for those in the church who refuse to mature and grow up, but it is not your job to tell them. It is your job to show them, by example, what being a Christian should look like.

The next step in our maturity is learning how to not be the source of conflict.

> *I am the Lord, your God, who teaches you what is best for you, who directs you in the way you should go. Isaiah 48:17*

Notice God's directions are for you. So you should not make what He tells you a mandate for others. Let God be their teacher and focus on your own walk with God.

When I see one of my children telling his sibling what he thinks is best, I ask him, "Who is the boss?" As he answers, "You are Mommy." It reminds him that he is not in charge. When we are tempted to tell others what to do, we need to ask ourselves, "Who is the boss?" Let God do His job.

If you do feel like God is leading you to guide others, remember that we are to be gentle, humble in heart and filled with a desire to help and encourage the other person. Don't attack a person with your judgment and then tack on God's name to it!

> *But in your hearts set apart Christ as Lord. Always be prepared to give an answer to everyone who asks you to give the reason for the hope that you have. But do this with gentleness and respect, keeping a clear conscience, so that those who speak maliciously against your good behavior in Christ may be ashamed of their slander.* 1 Peter 3:15-16

This verse encourages us to think about our responses before a conflict even takes place. Can we decide ahead of time that we will stop and think and not just react?

Even if we do all we can to not hurt others, I can guarantee that someone will still be offended but that is their immaturity and not yours. Let us simply make sure that our heart is clear before God.

Finally, so that we may mature, we need to work on our reactions.

As Jesus encouraged people to find rest in Him, he said the following:

> *Come to me all you who are weary and burdened, and I will give you rest. Take my yoke upon you and learn from me, for I am gentle and humble in heart, and you will find rest for your souls.* Matthew 11:28-29.

When people come to us with troubles, can we say that we are, "gentle and humble in heart" and can they find, "rest for their souls" as they share their troubles with us?

Have you heard the phrase, 'focus on the sin, not the sinner'? I can't judge the other person for I am a sinner. Only God can judge a person. We are all sinners. Yet through His word and by the help of the Holy Spirit, I can make a judgment on what is sin and what is not sin. Through God's strength, I can still love the person entangled in the sin and pray for them.

> *If you love those who love you, what credit is that to you? Even sinners love those who love them. And if you do good to those who are good to you, what credit is that to you? Even sinners do that. Luke 6:32-33*

Can we make a decision right now, that we are not going to let other people offend us? It really is a choice. With God's strength, we can choose not to be offended, angry or resentful. Yes, we can set boundaries but to hold onto bitterness will only hurt our own souls. We can choose to forgive and move on. It is in God's strength we can accomplish this, not on our own. But if we pray, He will help us in our responses to others.

We also need to realize that God is working in other people's lives, not just ours. God is always working in the hearts of mankind giving them the capacity to change. The person you were angry with years ago may have changed completely since you have last seen them. We need allow them the opportunity to change. And what about those people who never seem to change? We can safely leave the people that annoy us or hurt us in his care. Trust me, He sees everything and there is retribution for those who hurt his children.

> *Do not be deceived: God cannot be mocked. A man reaps what he sows. Galatians 6:7*

There's Always One in Every Family

I remember a time in the distant past when a well-known lady attended my church. She offended just about everyone she ever came in contact with. This is a story of one of my encounters with her.

We were at a fancy dinner event being held at the church. I was excited because I rarely had an opportunity to dress up when I was raising my little ones. I put on my best dress and styled my hair and went to church feeling beautiful.

When we arrived, my husband went to talk to some friends and this particular lady walked up to me with a smile. I said, "Hello" and was taken aback when she replied with: "Hello dear, it looks like you had to pour yourself into that dress."

Wow! I've never been knocked down so fast in my life! I mean, I know I had put on a bit of baby weight but I didn't even have to suck it in to zip up the dress, so I wasn't quite sure what she meant. I was so gutted. I just stood there speechless as she walked away. Later I was so thankful I was speechless because who knows what could have come out of my mouth at that moment!

I had recently made a commitment to God that I would choose to not be offended by other people. So I decided at that moment that I was not going to react. I had trained with God for this moment. I would do my best to ignore it and enjoy the rest of the evening. As I let it go, my emotions calmed down and I enjoyed the evening. This certainly was a better option than the old me replaying the movie reel over and over in my mind with the various responses I could have given to her. (Come on now, you know you've done it too!)

To my utter surprise, later that night she came over to me again and apologized! God had convicted her heart in a way that I could not. Who knows, maybe that night changed her level of maturity. But even if it didn't, I have to leave that to God because He was working on my maturity. This is where my faith in Him overrides my natural way of thinking.

> *But solid food is for the mature, who by constant use have trained themselves to distinguish good from evil. Hebrews 5:14*

Another time I was introduced to a lady at church that I had never met and she made it very clear, just after meeting me, that she didn't like me. How do you respond to something like that? I politely said I had to go and walked away. I couldn't think of anything that I had done to make her upset. So I prayed to God. I felt God asking me to pray for her and to bless her in various ways anonymously. He asked me to do nice things like send flowers and to give her little gifts. This was hard to do especially since she didn't know it was me that was trying to bless her.

> *But I said, "I have labored in vain; I have spent my strength for nothing at all. Yet what is due me is in the Lord's hand, and my reward is with my God." Isaiah 49:4*

I was about to join in a gossip session about her because there were a few other women that didn't like her either but I felt God chastise my heart. He reminded me that I was only to say something kind or to keep silent. I was reminded of a verse:

> *There is nothing concealed that will not be disclosed, or hidden that will not be made known. What you have said in the dark will be heard in the daylight, and what you have whispered in the ear in the inner rooms will be proclaimed from the roofs. Luke 12:2-3*

I never saw much of a change in her but by being obedient, I experienced a change in me. I am now free from the anxiety I used to have when I was around her. I love her with the love Christ has given to me and I want the best for her. That kind of blessing can only come from God!

> *"Therefore, as we have opportunity, let us do good to all people, especially to those who belong to the family of believers."*
> Galatians 6:10

As this verse specifies, we are to "do good" to all people. Then it emphasizes extra care for those who belong to the family of believers, Christians. Why do you think this is emphasized? Christians are some of the worst sinners and although Christ is actively working in their lives, it takes time. While they are on the journey to becoming what God has designed them to be, there is a whole lot of ugly that comes out in the process. Unfortunately, like any family, we experience the worst of each other in our own homes (or in this instance, the church)

It is very difficult to "do good" to all. I struggle with:

People who cut me off in traffic,
Someone who constantly puts me down,
Those I know who are not living in God's plan,
Selfish, ignorant people who say racist things or ask demeaning questions.

What about you? With whom do struggle to "do good"?

> *I, therefore, a prisoner for the Lord, urge you to walk in a manner worthy of the calling to which you have been called, with all humility and gentleness, with patience, bearing with one another in love, eager to maintain the unity of the Spirit in the bond of peace.* Ephesians 4:1-3 (ESV)

Although God is a master artist creating such unique and in-depth individuals, God knew it would be a struggle for all of us to get along. So why does He desire us to follow Jesus' example and do good to all people? Is it to change them or to better me? Is it to receive something in return from others or God? Is it for selfish reasons or to look good in front of others?

We are to "do good" to others to please the Lord. Yes, in doing good to others we feel good about ourselves. Yes, it boosts our confidence and helps us to be less self-focused and more concerned about the people around us. Yes, it helps us to steer clear of comparing ourselves with others. It has many benefits but all we need to be concerned about is that it pleases God. We are to live our lives only to please the Lord.

> *Am I now trying to win the approval of men, or of God? Or am I trying to please men? If I were still trying to please men, I would not be a servant of Christ. Galatians 1:10*

When we know who we are, people who make mistakes yet stand forgiven and free from shame, people who are loved by God no matter what we do, and as we replace comparison with "doing good" to all, we are learning to love others. As we learn to truly love others, we become better prepared for conflict.

Resolving Conflict

Once we prepare ourselves for conflict and we genuinely want to move forward in our difficult relationships, it's time to take action. So where do we start?

Jesus gave us three steps to follow to resolve conflict:

> *Then Jesus told his disciples, "If anyone would come after me, let him deny himself and take up his cross and follow me. Matthew 16:24*

Deny ourselves- when someone upsets you, don't give in to the first response that comes into your mind!

Take up our cross- Take this conflict and your issues to God and ask Him what He would have you do.
Follow Jesus- Look at the example of Jesus and ask yourself, what would He say or do? Follow His advice and example, written in the Bible.

Think to yourself, if this episode was recorded in the Bible, what would it say about the way I handled myself and those around me?

Love is looking past everything else to the person in need. It is making someone feel important because they are!

The book of Proverbs is filled with teachings on how to deal with conflict. It is found almost smack in the middle of the Bible and has one chapter for each day of the month. Coincidence? I think not. Take one chapter every day and study its teachings and you will gain much wisdom in dealing with relationships. Here are just a few teachings to get you started:

> *A gentle answer turns away wrath but a harsh word stirs up anger. Proverbs 15:1*

> *A tongue that brings healing is a tree of life, but a deceitful tongue crushes the spirit. Proverbs 15:4*

> *A patient man has great understanding, but a quick-tempered man displays folly. Proverbs 14:29*

> *There is a way that seems right to a man, but in the end it leads to death. Proverbs 14:12*

> *The fruit of that righteousness will be peace; its effect will be quietness and confidence forever. Isaiah 32:17*

If a relationship was broken a long time ago or a longstanding grudge has been held, as much as I would like to avoid any conflict, God usually convicts me to restore what I can with that person. Notice, who does the convicting? I must say here that God needs to convict you about restoration. There are some people that you simply need to stay away from due to abuse or other issues. Restoration in these cases may need to be brought about by a symbolic act.

How do I restore? Keep in mind the goal is to restore, not tear down. Pray about the situation. Ask God to help you to forgive and to release the other person into His care. Pray that God will work in the heart of the person you are struggling with. Cover every area that you can think of in prayer. Tell God everything that is on your mind.

Ask God if there are boundaries that you need to put into place to help you and to stop any form of abuse. Take the time you need to allow God to work in you and to speak to you.
Wait until you are ready before confronting anyone. You will know when it becomes the time to confront that person because you will not be angry and you will genuinely feel compassion for the person. You will be ready to act in love (remember sometimes it takes tough love)

> *If I speak in the tongues of men and of angels, but have not love, I am only a resounding gong or a clanging cymbal.*
>
> 1 Corinthians 13:1

When you act in love, you desire the very best for that person.

Finally, be prepared to face some hard truths about yourself. Often confronting others about something they did leads to a part that you played in that conflict. Remember your commitment to not be offended and take what is said to the Lord. If you need to change, He will help you. If you don't, He will release you. Simply apologize for the part you played in that conflict and ask for forgiveness. Your humility is powerful. Yet even if your humility is not appreciated by the other person, know that God sees it and will reward you. Also, you need to be prepared to pray with that person if the opportunity arises.

If you can come to the reconciliation table equipped with God's love and strength, you will be amazed at the outcome. Even if the other person leaves unchanged, I promise you, you will be changed in amazing ways.

Bringing about real restoration is never accomplished with a quick quip or a fleeting remorseful moment. Restoration requires God's help. Everyone feels indignation. It is how we deal with it, that concerns God.

> *Remember your word to your servant, for you have given me hope. My comfort in my suffering is this: Your promise preserves my life.*

> *The arrogant mock me unmercifully, but I do not turn from your law. I remember, Lord, your ancient laws and I find comfort in them. Indignation grips me because of the wicked, who have forsaken your law. Your decrees are the theme of my song wherever I lodge. Psalm 119: 49-54*

You will never be perfect at dealing with conflict. We all have our moments where we completely lose it. But what I have learned over and over again is that it's never too late to do the right thing. If you mess up and say some awful things, you can, with the strength of God, go back and apologize!

So go back and take a good hard look at yourself. Ask God to reveal any areas that you need to work on in your life to mature in the way you are meant to.

Be open to criticism yet wise in what you take on board. Examine your responses to criticism. Are they healthy responses?
Check your attitude. What does it look like in comparison to the chapter in 1 Corinthians 13? (Printed at the end of this chapter)

Begin to allow God to lead you in your responses to people and the timing of your responses. Learn to let go of other people's ugliness and instead "do good" to all. Let it define you rather than the culture around you. The result will bring so much freedom into your life.

Jesus spent His life teaching about forgiveness, restoring relationships with God and with others. God does everything in love, trying to get your heart in a place to receive that love. And it is all about relationships. It is so important to understand the concept of relationships in the way they were designed. Good relationships are God's design. So what's holding you back?

Love

If I speak in the tongues of men or of angels, but do not have love, I'm only a resounding gong or a clanging symbol. If I have the gift of prophecy and can fathom all mysteries and all knowledge, and if I have a faith that can move mountains, but I do not have love, I am nothing. If I get all I possess to the poor and give over my body to hardship that I may boast, but I do not have love, I gain nothing.

Love is patient, love is kind. It does not envy, it does not boast, it is not proud. It does not dishonor others, it is not self-seeking, it is not easily angry, it keeps no record of wrongs. Love does not delight in evil but rejoices with the truth. It always protects, always trusts, always hopes, always perseveres.

Love never fails. But where there are prophecies, they will cease; where there are tongues, they will be stilled; where there is knowledge, it will pass away. For we know in part and we prophesy in part, but when completeness comes, what is in part disappears. When I was a child, I talk like a child, I thought like a child, I reasoned like a child. When I became a man, I put the ways of childhood behind me. For now we see only a reflection as in a mirror; then we shall see face-to-face. Now I know in part; then I shall know fully, even as I am fully known.

And now these three remain: faith, hope and love. But the greatest of these is love.   1 Corinthians 13

Chapter 14
Fear Factor
What are you afraid of?

For God did not give us a spirit of timidity, but a spirit of power, of love and of self-discipline.
2 Timothy 1:7

Fear is a massive problem for humanity, yet most people are, ironically, afraid to talk about fear or deal with it. It's a powerful hidden danger to our lives. Unfortunately, the more you try to keep it hidden the more you feed its power. If you were to dig deep enough, you can't deny there is evil at its root. Like sin, there is no fear that is worse than another. We all experience fear in different ways but no matter who the person is, the fear is real and the experience is awful.

Now before we go any further, I will quickly mention that there is a healthy form of fear that I wish had a different name because the two can become confused. There is a reverent fear we have of God and those in authority positions. There is also a healthy fear that protects us from harming ourselves, like stopping us from jumping off a cliff or electrocuting ourselves. I want to make it clear that I am not addressing healthy fears because they're healthy, and we need them in our lives.

In the spiritual realm, Satan's way of immobilizing people, especially Christians, is through fear. He knows that fear grown to maturity can completely paralyze even the best of mankind. Fear is a designed evil meant to deceive us, warp our experiences and finally get us to doubt that God loves us and can save us.

Fear is inevitably the distraction that keeps you from something you are meant to do.

Fear keeps you from experiencing something amazing.

So let's talk about it and maybe even deal with the fear that currently resides in your life. I have found that if you struggle with fear as an adult, a good place to begin your journey of healing is to go back and face the fears of your childhood. It is a good idea to explore what was never talked about in your home and to look closely at the belief system that you developed about the challenges in your life. How did you cope with change? How did you deal with disappointments? Where did you go to find help? Where was your safe place?

Think back for a moment to when you were a kid. What was your first fear? How did you deal with it? If you were brave enough to tell someone, how did they react? Did you ever hear, "It's not real, it's only part of your imagination"?

As a side note, parents and mentors of children need to be aware that fear is something our children will have to face at some time and if we don't talk about it, how are we going to train them to deal effectively with their fears? Please take the time to listen to your children's fears and no matter how crazy they may seem, take the time to teach them how to deal with fear.

So what was my first fear? (Please note that what I am about to share with you breaks the best-known childhood code about dealing with fear: You're not supposed to tell anyone!) But the best way to deal with fear is to go back to where it started. So I tell you in the strictest of confidence about the very first fears I faced as a child.

Nearly every night as a child, especially when it was time to go to bed, I encountered my fear. When my parents had said their goodnights and left me alone in the room to go to sleep, a very strange thing happened in the dark. The toys on my shelf turned into faces and came to life! They were always looking at me and their mouths seemed to be moving but no sound came out. Even so, I seemed to know that whatever they were saying was something that I did not want to hear. In the daytime, they were just ordinary toys ranging from books, stuffed animals, dolls and knick-knacks. How they changed so clearly into faces perplexed me. When I turned on the lights, however, they went straight back to being the toys that I knew they were.

When my parents went out for the night and I was with a babysitter (and even when I was old enough to stay on my own), I began to see what I call shadow men. They were about 3 feet tall and darted about the place but usually poked their heads around the corners. Although they were shadows, they were often white and they didn't have any features. Their hands didn't have fingers and their faces were blank. It was as if I would see them out of the corner of my eye and then when I looked, they would disappear. They never said or did anything really, but it was the fact that I knew they were around the house, hiding.

I also disliked and feared clown pictures, especially ones with emotions or teardrops running from their eyes. I refused to even look at the pictures as I thought they might come to life right in the frame!

And if all that wasn't enough, I also had other fears, like something living under the bed waiting to grab my ankles when I had to go to the toilet in the middle of the night. It was usually this fear that stopped me from running to my parents' room for help at night.

If I ever did make it to the toilet, I was afraid to look into the mirror, in case I saw someone else looking back at me. Credit for that one goes to friends who had seen it in a movie and one day decided it would be fun to dare each other to stand alone in the bathroom to see if it was true.

Not surprisingly, I often had very vivid and terrifying nightmares. I can even remember some of them today, that's how clear and real they were to me!

Although most of these fears I knew were part of my imagination (or were they?), it didn't stop them from existing. It also did not stop me from being a normal kid in the daytime. As I said, no one knew that these things happened to me at night so no one knew any different. After a while, I got used to seeing things at night and I just tried to ignore them. They didn't go away though for a long time.

So why am I bringing them up now? Well, I find it interesting that when I did muster up the courage to tell someone, to break the code and talk about my past fears, I found I was not alone! Although fears differ from person to person, I am amazed at how similar my experiences were to my friends and family.

One day when I filled in at a school as a substitute teacher somehow the subject of fear came up. It was a Christian private school and I was in a class made up of mainly ten to twelve-year-olds. I wondered how many kids suffered the way I did from fears. I asked how many of them had ever seen their toys come to life at night. Nearly every hand went up in the classroom! Wow, I didn't expect that!

I then asked how many suffered from nightmares? Just over half of the class raised their hands. When I asked how many of them had told their parents about the problem, I think there were only about two or three hands that went up. And only one child had been given any sort of instruction with how to deal with their nighttime fears.

It is these childhood fears that start a process of the way we deal (or don't deal) with fear as adults. Fears develop and change over time. Thinking that it is too silly to mention to anyone else, fears remain hidden deep within the psyche and fester. These fears get in the way of what life is really meant to be like. Fear can potentially paralyze but fear will attempt to cripple our spirit in some way.

Now whenever I get the opportunity, I like to talk to kids about their fears and nightmares. Here is the advice I give them:

Just as a switch of the light disperses the darkness around you, when you bring light to your fears it diminishes their power over you. How do you bring fears into the light?

1. Talk about your fears with close friends or family and ask them to pray for you.
2. Examine your fears and pray that God helps you to understand where they stemmed from.
3. Find out about Jesus Christ. He is the only one who has power over all fears. Read what the Bible says about fear.

As we get older our fears become more complex and sometimes difficult to distinguish from other feelings. But the process of dealing with them is still the same.

So let's pull out some of these fears from the hidden recesses of darkness into the light. It's always easier to examine someone else's fears rather than our own, so we will look at some of the people from the Bible as a reference for the various fears. We will start with Peter, a disciple of Jesus to discuss our first fear:

Fear of Man

Peter hung around Jesus every day and he saw and experienced his miracles first hand. He even walked on water with the guy! He loved Jesus as a friend and a brother but also saw something many people missed. The more time that he spent with Jesus, he began to see that Jesus was the Son of God.

At their last supper together, Jesus explained His imminent and impending death. Jesus told his close companions that he must do this alone. Yet Peter, filled with confidence at the time, felt differently.

> *Peter asked, 'Lord, why can't I follow you now? I will lay down my life for you.'*
>
> *Jesus answered, 'Will you really lay down your life for me? I tell you the truth before the rooster crows, you will disown me three times!" John 13:37-38.*

Peter truly did love Jesus. He believed that if the opportunity arose, he would even lay down his life for Jesus. Yet, just as Jesus prophesied, Peter later denied even knowing him, on three separate occasions. So what happened to take the Peter, filled with confidence and boldness, to the Peter who would deny even knowing Jesus?

Fear of Man set in. Peter's love for Jesus had him hanging around the courts to find out what was happening. Yet as things started to turn ugly and accusations were beginning to fly around, fear began to set in. People were asking questions and started to accuse Peter of being a supporter of the now condemned man, Jesus. Peter was confused and embarrassed. He didn't know how to respond under the pressure of pointing fingers so he acted like he didn't know Jesus. When asked if he knew Jesus, he denied it. When asked a third time, upon Peter's denial, Jesus looked at him from across the courtyard.

> *About an hour later another asserted, "Certainly this fellow was with him, for he is a Galilean."*
>
> *Peter replied, 'Man, I don't know what you're talking about!' Just as he was speaking, the rooster crowed. The Lord turned and looked straight at Peter. Then Peter remembered the word the Lord had spoken to him: "Before the rooster crows today, you will disown me three times." And he went outside and wept bitterly. Luke 22:60-62*

When I read this, I just cringe. I don't want to think about the many times that I have disowned Christ. I love Jesus with all of my heart. Yet sometimes I say and do things that knowingly or unknowingly show otherwise. This story is not just about Peter, it's about all of us. So many times, we deny who we are in fear of what others may think of us.

Peter's disappointment lay only within. He only has himself to blame. He goes out and weeps. Satan is quick to move in with shame and guilt. Peter can't forgive himself. He is immobilized.

There were probably several fears that Peter faced in the early hours of that morning but certainly, the fear of what those around him would do to him if they found out he was following the man on trial was one of the big ones. The Fear Of Man is a powerful fear. Peter thought he would do anything for Jesus but when questioned under pressure by others, fear overtook desire. He was watching horrible things happening to Jesus. If Peter claimed that he knew Jesus, who knows what would happen to him?

Fear of Man has stopped me from doing many things. For me just imagining the thoughts of others can immobilize me. Past memories flood into my mind of the times when others hurt me verbally or emotionally. I become fearful that they may happen again.

The Fear of Man has stopped me from developing and displaying my gifts. Things like singing, playing music and speaking in front of others. Fear of man has stopped me from standing up for myself or others when confronted by rude and hurtful people. Fear of Man has stopped important conversations that could bring others to healing and finding God. Fear of Man has stopped me from believing in myself when deep down, I know that I can do it.

> *The LORD is with me; I will not be afraid. What can man do to me? Psalm 118:6*

Jesus victoriously rose from the dead and visited the disciples several times. Jesus forgave Peter but Peter couldn't forgive himself. Although Jesus already knows of Peter's great love for him, He asks Peter three times to declare that love, canceling out the three times that Peter denied Jesus.

> *"The Lord is my light and my salvation – whom shall I fear?*
> *The Lord is the stronghold of my life – of whom shall I be afraid?"*
> *Psalm 27:1*

Jesus always knows just what we need to pick us up out of our failure and fear and place us back on the road we were originally meant to travel. Peter not only receives Jesus' forgiveness, but he also receives the power to forgive himself. What happens next? Peter is freed from the Fear of Man and boldly goes out and teaches about Jesus and His forgiveness from his own experience.

> *Fear of man will prove to be a snare, but whoever trusts in the LORD is kept safe. Proverbs 29:25*

If you have been hurt and fearful of man I want to pray right now for you:

> *Lord, only you know the hurt buried deep within us. Be with us and protect us as we examine past relationships that have caused pain. Help us to see things clearly so that we can let go of the things we were not responsible for and deal with the things we were.*
>
> *May we experience you in a new and powerful way as we face our* Fear of Man. *Help us to begin living the dreams we tucked away long ago.*
>
> *Please create within us a new sense of self-worth based on your truth. Deliver us from this fear so that we can be free to be the people you have called us to be. Give us the courage to*

dream big and use the gifts and talents we have to change the world. For those who feel bound by this fear, I pray you will release them now in your Holy Name, Jesus. Amen

Fear of Failure

There is another fear that causes many people to stop short of achieving the dreams God placed in their hearts and that is the **Fear of Failure**. Usually, this fear has a prerequisite of a "good-intentioned" failure experience. Let's look at Moses' story for an example of this.

The Egyptian woman that raised Moses as her adopted Hebrew son, was the daughter of Pharaoh. This is the same Pharaoh that is described as having:

> *dealt treacherously with (the Israelites) and oppressed our forefathers by forcing them to throw out their newborn babies so that they would die. Acts 7:19*

As Moses grew older, he saw the great injustice of the Hebrew people being forced into slavery. Although he was raised in the royal palace of the people causing that injustice, in his heart he knew to treat people so cruelly, was wrong.

> *One day, after Moses had grown up, he went out to where his own people were and watched them at their hard labor. He saw an Egyptian beating a Hebrew, one of his own people. Looking this way and that and seeing no one, he killed the Egyptian and hid him in the sand. Exodus 2:11-12*

Wow, that was not the best response to social injustice! However, Moses was in the heat of the moment and something had to be done. None of us knows how we would respond given the same circumstances. Moses tried to do the right thing, failed miserably, ran back to the palace and hoped the problem would sort itself out.

The story continues:

> *The next day he went out and saw two Hebrews fighting. He asked the one in the wrong, "Why are you hitting your fellow Hebrew?"*
>
> *The man said who made you ruler and judge over us? Are you thinking of killing me as you killed the Egyptian?*
>
> *Then Moses was afraid and thought, "What I did must have become known." Exodus 2: 13-14*

Not only did Moses mess up, now he was caught out.

> *Moses thought that his own people would realize that God was using him to rescue them, but they did not. Acts 7:25*

Moses' actions were intended to help the people of Israel, God's people. He was trying to follow a calling, a purpose placed in his heart by God.

It was no accident that Moses, with a Hebrew heritage, was saved from death and raised in an Egyptian royal palace. We sense that God had a purpose and a plan for Moses all along to save the people of Israel. Yet, when it becomes known about his mistake, the Fear of Failure sets in. In another setting, he may have been painted a hero for starting a revolt against the Egyptians, yet, because of the comment of one man, he felt a failure.

Moses' did what I and so many do best. Moses ran away! He fled and fear settled into his heart. God led Moses into a safe place to allow him time to heal. God always knows exactly what we need to recover from a failure. Moses was accepted into a wonderful family. He got married and had a son. Later when the time was right, God spoke to Moses personally through a bush that flamed with fire yet was never consumed. God spoke and reminded Moses of what he was created for. God's calling on Moses from the very beginning was to be a great leader.

God said, *"So now, go. I am sending you to Pharaoh to bring my people the Israelites out of Egypt."* (You can read all of what God said to Moses in Exodus Chapters 3 and 4.)

Instead of feeling empowered by God's mission, Moses fires off questions that begin to turn into angry statements revealing his Fear of Failure. You can imagine, the movie reel of his past failure playing over and over in his mind as he questions God:

> *"Who am I, that I should go to Pharaoh and bring the Israelites out of Egypt?"*

> *"Suppose I go to the Israelites and say to them, 'The God of your fathers has sent me to you,' and they ask me, 'What is his name?' Then what shall I tell them?"*

> *"What if they do not believe me or listen to me and say, 'The Lord did not appear to you?'"*

> *"O Lord, I have never been eloquent, neither in the past nor since you have spoken to your servant. I am slow of speech and tongue."*

The Lord answers him:

> *Who gave human beings their mouths? Who makes them deaf or mute? Who gives them sight or makes them blind? Is it not I, The*

> *Lord? Now go: I will help you speak and will teach you what to say.*

God had spoken and His word is final. End of argument. Right? The argument should have ended there. But then Moses took it one step further:

> *"O Lord, please send someone else to do it."*

It is at this point that God gets angry.

> *Then the Lord's anger burned against Moses. Exodus 4:14*

Let me ask you a very important question. Why do you think the Lord was angry with Moses? Was it because he questioned God?

No, the Bible shows example after example that God loves to answer our questions. He lovingly answered similar questions that arose from the fears of Abraham, Jacob, Mary, Thomas and many others who were called by God to do what seemed impossible. God is filled with love and compassion. He understands our humanness.

The Lord's anger only burned when Moses' questions turned into a statement that he did not want to do what God was asking. Because of his Fear of Failure, Moses doubted. He doubted God's power and divinity. He doubted that God could use him. He made a strong statement to his creator that the creation wasn't good enough.

Nothing raises God's anger more than those who don't believe that every human being is special to God, designed with love and care and with God's help is capable to do just about anything. Yes, that means you too!

The key to overcoming the Fear of Failure is to go to God and ask Him to reveal to you just how special you are. Once you know who you are in God, you will not need to fear failure. You can simply be all that God wants you to be and that is a success, even if those around you view it as a failure. This also squashes any doubts that we will never be good enough to fulfill God's calling upon our lives.

Even when I think I have blown it, God has used my mistakes to help others. God has also used other people's mistakes to help me. Mistakes and "failures" refine us. If we continue to learn from them, we will eventually make less of them and their impact decreases. Turn every mistake into a lesson. Remember, whatever it is that you fear you may fail, is most likely the very thing God wants you to succeed at.

If you have the Fear of Failure, let me pray for you now:

> Lord, you created each of us uniquely with a specific purpose. We are very special and deeply loved! As we read the Bible, please reveal this deep love you have for us. Help us to see that the Fear of Failure is designed by Satan to stop us from living out our calling. I pray that just like Moses, Help us to trust you as we step out into new callings and do great things.
>
> Give us a good sense of humor and the ability to laugh at ourselves without any condemning thoughts. Refine us through our mistakes and use us to show others that it's okay to make them. When others fail, I pray that we will be quick to go and stand by their side and encourage them to get back up again. For those who feel bound by this fear, I pray God will release them now from this fear as only He can do. Amen.

Fear of the Unknown

When thinking about the Fear of the Unknown, Joshua, the successor of Moses, springs to mind. When Moses died, imagine having to be the one to follow in his footsteps! Moses confronted his fears, faced the Pharaoh, did amazing miracles of God and delivered the entire nation of Israel out of Egypt, despite the hostile forces around him. With God's help, he spoke boldly and performed miracles by God's hand. Moses left to be with his God forever and suddenly Joshua is now responsible for the entire nation of Israel and their future.

Joshua is called to lead the Israelites into the new land in which God has destined for them. No pressure, right? Joshua had to face the **Fear of the Unknown**.

On the outside Joshua looks calm and in control as he commands the armies to do as God asks, to take the land that was rightfully theirs. So how do I know that Joshua had to deal with the Fear of the Unknown?

First, Joshua was about to start a war. Second, look at what words and phrases God is continually speaking to him and over him.

> *Be strong and very courageous. Be careful to obey all the law my servant Moses gave you; do not turn from it to the right or to the left, that you may be successful wherever you go. Do not let this Book of the Law depart from your mouth; meditate on it day and night, so that you may be careful to do everything written in it. Then you will be prosperous and successful.*
>
> *Have I not commanded you? Be strong and courageous. Do not be terrified; do not be discouraged, for the Lord your God will be with you wherever you go. Joshua 1:7-9*

God reassured Joshua (and us) to not be fearful but strong and courageous. God then gave Joshua some very important instructions that would help him to succeed no matter what the future would bring.

Joshua saw Moses as both strong and courageous. But remember Moses wasn't always that way. He was the one that ran away and hid for many years, questioned God directly and refused to speak on God's behalf. But then, as he got to know the living God and to do what God asked of him, Moses became strong and courageous. And that is exactly how we can become strong and courageous too, by getting to know God and doing what He says. What better way to get to know God than to read the Bible?

Yet, God wants us to do more than just read the Bible, He wants us to study it, meditate upon its words and to do what is written in it. It is only when we apply what we learn and walk out our faith in daily life that we become stronger and more courageous.

I've always been a deep thinker, an 'old soul' with a melancholy personality. A fear that I have often wrestled with is the Fear of the Unknown. Like most people, I want to know what to expect. Change brings stress, even when the changes are good. Why is that? Because we know that right after the change there is something unknown.

I used to always worry about all of the unknowns the future would bring. When I first began a relationship with the living God, I struggled a lot. I mean, is there a change more monumental than handing everything over to God and allowing Him to be in control? What will He do? How will He do it? Where will He ask me to go? What will He ask me to do?

He also leads us into the deep unknown areas within. Who am I? Why was I created? What secrets or sins am I hiding? Where will I go when I die? What does eternity look like?

So how did I overcome this fear? By following the same instructions that God gave to Joshua. I had to ask God to help me to overcome my pride issues and to look beyond what is deemed by the world as common sense. I had to decide in my heart that I would be open to instruction. Then I meditated on His Word, prayed and listened. I held onto my faith that God would answer and He did. I began to understand that He is always with me, no matter if I feel it or not.

The more I stepped out into the unknown, simply trusting that God would lead and guide me, the more I experienced the powerful presence of God. I do not doubt in my mind that God is real and He is with me. Now I look forward to the unknown because I know God is going to do something exciting in my life.

For me, stepping out into the unknown has brought such a blessing, that I would have never had dreamed of having. Growing up, I was simply a number. To be specific, I was number 635 out of 725 students in my high school in Ohio. When I went to find my picture in the class photo, it wasn't even there! They forgot to include me... Sigh.

Yet, by following God's instructions, I have been able to do amazing things with my life. A few highlights include: moving to Australia from America to start a beautiful family with my husband, overcoming an eating disorder, navigating through bureaucratic red tape so we could adopt the most amazing son one could ever wish for, having breakfast with the Prime Minister of Australia, traveling the world with my family, writing books, speaking and running conferences and experiencing life in so many ways I never dreamed of. Yet all of these fade in comparison to the moments I have been in the presence of the Lord and have heard him speak to me.

As you come to know your purpose in life, who you are and where you are going, you will begin to conquer the Fear of the Unknown.

If you Fear the Unknown, let me pray for you now:

> *Lord, no one knows what tomorrow will bring but we can be certain that our future is in good hands when we entrust it to you. Help us now to have that kind of trust because we are*

unable to maintain it by ourselves. I pray against any anxiety, worry or depression caused by this fear. Help us to walk forward. Give us hope for tomorrow. Give us the courage we need to face what we can't see. For those who feel bound by Fear of the Unknown, I pray you will release them now in your Holy Name, Jesus Amen.

Fear of Losing Control

We make so many decisions each day that we can tend to think that we are in control of our lives. We do to a limited extent, thanks to the grace given by God but ultimately, you can make the best of plans and the story can take a completely different turn. Let's look at the story of Naaman:

> *Naaman was commander of the army of the king of Aram. He was a great man in the sight of his master and highly regarded, because through him the Lord had given victory to Aram.*
>
> *He was a valiant soldier, but he had leprosy.* 2 Kings 5:1

As a commander, Naaman was used to control. No one wanted to have leprosy, but to someone who likes to be in control of life, it must have been a huge blow. After some time, a servant girl taken captive from Israel told Naaman's wife about a prophet in Israel who could heal diseases such as leprosy. His name was Elisha.

When Naaman heard this, he went straight away to the king to get permission to see this prophet. The king granted permission and Naaman set out on a journey filled with hope. When he arrived:

> *Naaman went with his horses and chariots and stopped at the door of Elisha's house. Elisha sent a messenger to say to him, "Go, wash yourself seven times in the Jordan, and your flesh will be restored and you will be cleansed."*

> *But Naaman went away angry and said, "I thought that he would surely come out to me and stand and call on the name of the Lord his God, wave his hand over the spot and cure me of my leprosy. Are not Abana and Pharpar, the rivers of Damascus, better than all the waters of Israel? Couldn't I wash in them and be cleansed?" So he turned and went off in a rage.* 2 Kings 5:9-12

Namaan probably spent most of his long journey imagining this moment. He wanted it to play out in the way that he planned it in his mind. However, when he arrived, the amazing prophet of God didn't even come out to see him but sent a messenger instead. What a blow to both Naaman's ideas and his pride. After all, he was a servant in the royal palace, first in line to the king. Naaman didn't know it, but underneath all of his planning, lay a deep-seated fear, the **Fear of Losing Control**.

Naaman left in a rage and would have gone home the same as he came, with leprosy. Thankfully, his servants intervened:

> *Naaman's servants went to him and said, "My father, if the prophet had told you to do some great thing, would you not have done it? How much more, then, when he tells you, 'Wash and be cleansed'!" So he went down and dipped himself in the Jordan seven times, as the man of God had told him, and his flesh was restored and became clean like that of a young boy.*
>
> 2 Kings 5:13-14

Naaman had to accept that things were not going to go as he planned. Yet, the new plan held life, healing and freedom. Thankfully, he was convinced to follow it. The new plan changed his life forever, healing him not only of leprosy but of much deeper problems such as pride, manipulation and control issues.

As we hear constant news reports of natural disasters, human disasters and generally horrible things happening every moment around the world, it's easy to see why our daily fears can turn into life enveloping fears. Many people don't realize this underlying Fear of Losing Control.

This fear is very subtle and therefore, hard to see or to admit having it. Back when my children were young, I would reluctantly take them to the grocery store with me. Let's just say they were at the age of determining boundaries. I already had to stop the car because my son threw his shoe at my head while I was driving. As we parked my daughter had to go to the toilet. I knew from experience, we would not make it to the public bathrooms so I pulled out the little red potty from the back of my car and sat her down right there in the parking lot. Yes, I got a few looks from those passing by.

When I arrived at the store, I was already exhausted from the drive. Amazingly this day, I made it through the aisles and even checked out before my son decided to throw what looked like an epic tantrum. There was nothing I could do except to just be there for him. Well after a few seconds, I began to see the glares from other people. They would shake their heads in disapproval as they walked by. I could hear them muttering under their breath, in a not so subtle way, that I should control my children. What could I do? Little did anyone know that my son had autism and that certain noises, smells and situations would set him off. But does it matter? Just a few days before, my daughter did the same thing over not getting a toy that she wanted. Am I a better parent in either situation?

Why are we so quick to cast the blame onto parents, especially when we are parents ourselves? This type of scenario could have happened to any of us. Regardless of parenting, children have a mind of their own and will often do things that parents do not authorize! (We can only do our best, pray to God and hope for the best.)

I see this parent guilt trip played out just about every day in the grocery store when children are crying or throwing temper tantrums, at school when someone's child gets an award and on sporting fields when a child either wins or loses a game. The truth be told, we don't want to address the fear that we have no more control over our child than anyone else. So we take pride that our child is doing the right thing, at this moment in time.

Yes, as parents we have an influence but we do not have the ultimate control over our children or their behavior. If we did, we would stifle any intellectual or artistic freedom that child might bring into our world. If we could think about this we would come to know God and His purpose for us as His children.

The Fear of Losing Control can be found in many places: health fanatics who fear anything from aging to illness, over-possessive parents/friends/spouses who fear someone will leave, Dooms-Dayers who fear the end of the world, even our children who fear going outside to play because they've been taught by society that any evil seen on the news could happen to them and that global warming and pollution have destroyed our earth.

For all the control freaks out there, those who think they are in control and even those who think others are controlling them: There is only One who is in control and it's not you, nor anyone around you. Listen as God speaks to mankind:

> Where were you when I laid the earth's foundation? Tell me, if you understand. Who marked off its dimensions? Surely you know! Who stretched a measuring line across it? On what were its footings set, or who laid its cornerstone- while the morning stars sang together and all the angels shouted for joy?
>
> Can you bring forth constellations in their seasons or lead out the Bear with its cubs? Do you know the laws of the heavens?

> Can you raise your voice to the clouds and cover yourself with a flood of water? Do you send the lightning bolts on their way? Do they report to you, 'Here we are'?
>
> Do you know when the mountain goats give birth? Do you watch when the doe bears her fawn? Do you count the months till they bear? Do you know the time they give birth? Job 38:4-7, 32-35 & 39:1-2

I'm not sure what control you think you have, but the hard truth is that you've never had it and you never will.

> All the days ordained for me were written in your book before one of them came to be. Psalm 139:16

Are we to be fearful that we are not in control? No, God wants us to be comforted by the knowledge that He is in control of everything and if you will place your trust in Him, He will disperse the fears you have. The good news is that once we realize we have no control and begin to trust in the one who does hold control, we can let go. Think about it, why do children enjoy life more than adults? They are not controlled by their worries. They trust their needs will be met and this brings such freedom and joy. When we are under the wings of the Lord's protection, we have nothing to fear.

> There is no wisdom, no insight, no plan that can succeed against the Lord. Proverbs 21:30

This is why it is so crucial to understand God's will and purpose for your life. If it is not part of His plan for you, it will not succeed. It doesn't matter how much control you think you have. You will work and work, get frustrated, think you are making some progress only to fall and feel defeated. However, when we give way to God's plans, we find that His plans aren't so bad after all. They bring life and freedom.

If you have a Fear of Losing Control, let me pray for you now:

> *Lord, it is hard to admit that we don't have control of the situations around us. Yet, You do. Help us to know you more intimately so that we can trust you. Give us the strength we need to trust you with our children, our families, our jobs and our future.*
>
> *When we face discouragement, I pray Lord that You will remind us to talk to you about everything. I pray against anxiety and worry and instead ask for peace and contentment in our souls. Help us to stop comparing ourselves to anyone else, so that we may be content with who we are and what we have. Help us to not judge others but rather show compassion and encouragement. We thank you that You are in control and we can release our* Fear of Losing Control *into Your hands, Amen.*

Fear of Evil

We can't deny there is evil in the world today and it comes in all forms. Jesus saw evil as well.

> *When Jesus got out of the boat, a man with an impure spirit came from the tombs to meet him. This man lived in the tombs, and no one could bind him anymore, not even with a chain. For he had often been chained hand and foot, but he tore the chains apart and broke the irons on his feet. No one was strong enough to subdue him. Night and day among the tombs and in the hills he would cry out and cut himself with stones.*
> *Mark 5:2-5*

Here was a man who was possessed by impure spirits. It doesn't state how this happened but it was clear that people were terrified of him. We read later in the passage there were possibly thousands of evil spirits in this man. He was unmanageable. He hurt others and himself.

There's no denying evil exists. In the spiritual, we call it demonic or satanic. If welcomed, it is powerful and dark. It holds power that we as humans can't compete with. Although it is often glorified today through television shows and movies, for those feeling oppressed by evil it can be a terrifying fear. It may seem that there is no way out. Many are bound by the **Fear of Evil.**

However, I want to make clear that demonic beings are not in equal opposition to God. God created all spiritual beings. They are subject to His will. Just the name of Jesus is powerful enough to disperse evil in a moment. If we know God, we need not fear evil.

Notice what happens to the demon-possessed man when Jesus comes on the scene.

> *When he saw Jesus from a distance, he ran and fell on his knees in front of him. He shouted at the top of his voice, "What do you want with me, Jesus, Son of the Most High God? In God's name don't torture me!" For Jesus had said to him, "Come out of this man, you impure spirit!" Mark 5:6-8*

For a long time, I was haunted by the Fear of Evil. I experienced horrible nightmares and felt the oppression of dark spirits. Many times in the middle of the night, I felt an unwelcome presence in my room. It seemed to be all-encompassing yet it felt as if it was sitting on my chest, making it difficult to breathe or call out. Occasionally, I experienced a similar feeling in the middle of the day and felt frozen to my seat unable to move. I have also seen evil spirits surface in other people and in places of residence. When I experienced evil, I felt powerless to do anything or tell anyone.

For anyone experiencing the Fear of Evil, there is only one answer and that is found in the power that comes in calling upon the name of Jesus Christ. There is power in His name because demonic beings know the authority that backs it up.

If you are struggling with the demonic realm, you need a Savior. Freedom from this fear is simple yet satan will have you believe it's impossible. If you are serious about finding freedom, you will need to pray to God and ask Him to be the Lord of your life. There is no other power that can break the hold of demonic footholds in your life.

If you are struggling with the Fear of Evil or feel that you are tormented by evil and you want to be free forever, pray the following prayer out loud:

> *Lord, I ask for your Holy Presence to cleanse my spirit of any evil. I ask forgiveness for my sins and humbly ask you now to be the Lord of my life. Please give me the strength to turn away from any evil in my life and to stop any sinful practices in which I am involved.*
>
> *By the authority and power of Jesus Christ, I bind any demonic spirits and cast them out of my life and my home. I renounce any evil I have allowed in my life. I will no longer believe the lies of the enemy. Thank you that you have taken my sin away from me by dying in my place and given me life conquering death permanently. By your grace, I have been set free.*
>
> *Please help me to find a Godly church that teaches your truths and other Christians who can help me on this journey. Protect me and keep me safe in your care. In the name Jesus Christ, I pray, Amen.*

If you are a Christian and wrestle with a Fear of Evil, you need to take a close look at what you are feeding your soul. As I tell my children, you cannot "un-see" something. Once it's seen, it's in there. What type of shows or movies are you watching?

> *I will walk in my house with a blameless heart. I will set before my eyes no vile thing. The deeds of faithless men I hate; they will not cling to me. Men of perverse heart shall be far from me; I will have nothing to do with evil. Psalm 101:2-4*

If you hang out with people who think it's fun to be malicious towards others, again it seeps into your soul. You may have heard the phrase, "Garbage in, garbage out." What's been coming out of your mouth? Do you speak of love, justice and praise of God or do you speak evil of others, tell lies and make fun of people around you? If you participate in sin of any kind, you open the door for evil to enter into your soul.

Evil can and does exist within us. We need to be quick to repent of our sins and submit our souls to God on a daily so that sin will not take root in our lives. Anyone of us is capable of giving into evil in an instant. Look at the story of Cain, the first son mentioned in the Bible and Abel his younger brother. Cain was a farmer and Abel a shepherd. They both brought an offering to the Lord.

> *The Lord looked with favor on Abel and his offering, but on Cain and his offering, He did not look with favor. So Cain was very angry, and his face was downcast.*
>
> *Then the Lord said to Cain, "Why are you angry? Why is your face downcast? If you do what is right, will you not be accepted? But if you do not do what is right, sin is crouching at your door; it desires to have you, but you must rule over it."*
> *Genesis 4:2-7*

Cain did not bring the correct offering. When God didn't approve, he became angry and upset. God gave him instructions on how to make it right and warned him of the sin that was within him. God had given Cain exactly what he needed to overcome his sin but

Cain gave in to his anger and took matters into his own hands. He was full of pride and decided to ignore God. By allowing sin to reign in his life, he opened the door for evil to move through him.

> *While they were in the field, Cain attacked his brother Abel and killed him. Genesis 4:8*

In a moment's decision, Cain gave anger free reign and murdered his own brother! Notice the ripple effects of one man's evil. Cain's anger affected his parents, his relationship with God and the future of what would have been, had Abel not been killed. Giving into his anger didn't just affect his life but the lives of everyone around him. That's how evil works. Just one evil decision can affect thousands of lives.

> *Be self-controlled and alert. Your enemy the devil prowls around like a roaring lion looking for someone to devour. Resist him, standing firm in the faith. 1 Peter 5:8*

That's why we see so many Christian people, who are highly regarded as godly people, fall into sin. Unfortunately, anyone is capable of falling into the sins of addiction, pornography, adultery and even completely denying that God exists at all. The downfall of Christians impacts the faith of so many people around them, causing some to walk away from the faith forever. As Christians, we should not be quick to judge but rather pray that we don't fall into temptation ourselves.

Let's pray now:

> Lord, we thank you for what you have accomplished on the cross for us. We thank you for the forgiveness of our sins and our eternal salvation.
>
> We want to confess that we have not obeyed you and your word. We have allowed sin back into our lives and have not

been living in a way that pleases you. Forgive us now and help us to not only repent of our sins but to walk away from them. We pray for our brothers and sisters in Christ, that have fallen into sinful ways. Please protect them and restore them to a right relationship with you. Deliver us all from the Fear of Evil.

Give us the strength to seek you daily and to not judge others for what we could easily do ourselves. We renounce any footholds we have given the devil and ask your Holy Spirit to cleanse our souls from any evil. Help us to live in a way that honors you.

In Jesus name, we pray, Amen.

Fear of Death

Finally, we reach what is seemingly the biggest fear of all, the **Fear of Death.** Although all fears are equally horrible, this particular fear is the one that people revert to when someone asks, "What's the worst thing that can happen?"

In the world, death can only be seen through the human perspective. Often it is portrayed as evil or bad. The words that surround death are full of darkness: black, grim reaper, loss, finality and sadness. It leaves a sense of being alone and that there is no one around who can help you. You can keep ignoring it or pushing it aside but at some point, every person must face the issue of death.

The Fear of Death quietly hides behind most other fears. It can grip your heart and rip in half. Death steals our loved ones and leaves us feeling gutted. It robs us of time and experiences. It's never fair. It leaves behind questions and dreams cut short. It causes sorrow and grief beyond measure.

It was around the issue of death that we see Jesus moved to weep for those he loved. Jesus was the only human that truly understood what lay behind the curtain of death. Yet His heart broke for the sorrow of those around Him and for the state of the world when it got off course from the original plan.

> *When Mary reached the place where Jesus was and saw him, she fell at his feet and said, "Lord, if you had been here, my brother would not have died."*
>
> *When Jesus saw her weeping, and the Jews who had come along with her also weeping, he was deeply moved in spirit and troubled. "Where have you laid him?" he asked.*
>
> *"Come and see, Lord," they replied.*
>
> *Jesus wept. Luke 11:32-35*

I think Jesus felt so deeply the sorrow of humanity. His creation just could not understand the freedom and life that were available to them. They didn't know Jesus well enough to understand what He was trying to say to them. His people were blinded by the deception of death. They were afraid. Jesus was not. It was the reason He came from the heavenly realm into our human realm. Jesus came to bring life.

> *Then Jesus said, "Did I not tell you that if you believe, you will see the glory of God?"*
>
> *So they took away the stone. Then Jesus looked up and said, "Father, I thank you that you have heard me. I knew that you always hear me, but I said this for the benefit of the people standing here, that they may believe that you sent me."*
>
> *When he had said this, Jesus called in a loud voice, "Lazarus, come out!" The dead man came out, his hands and feet wrapped with strips of linen, and a cloth around his face. Luke 11:40-44*

Jesus spoke the words that brought life back into Lazarus' human body. He didn't struggle or have difficulty in doing this. Jesus spoke and even death had to bow to His command.

I'm not sure that Lazarus would have been as excited as his family at his return to this earth. The Bible doesn't record his response. The Bible doesn't speak much of death, for the one who finds Jesus, finds life and will never experience death. It is truly good news in a world of bad news.

Overcoming this fear requires a closeness with Jesus that can only come from interacting with Him regularly. When you become intimately close with your Savior, He will lead you down a path where you will move through and beyond this fear.

Yet, for those who ask God to lead their lives, the end is the most beautiful part. As God has promised to never leave us, we will never be alone. your physical life may end but the soul continues to live and what lies ahead is worthy of a celebration rather than grieving. Consider the following verses:

> I tell you the truth, whoever hears my word and believes him who sent me has eternal life and will not be condemned; he has crossed over from death to life. John 5:24

> He will wipe every tear from their eyes. There will be no more death or mourning or crying or pain, for the old order of things has passed away. Revelation 21:4

> When the perishable has been clothed with the imperishable, and the mortal with immortality, then the saying that is written will come true; "Death has been swallowed up in victory." "Where, O death, is your victory? Where O death, is your sting?"
> 1 Corinthians 15: 54-55

Being a deep thinker, I've struggled with this fear many times myself. The more I thought about the foreverness of death and eternity, the more frightened I became. Yet, the more that I came to know who I am in Christ, the less grip this fear has on me. As I come into the presence of God in worship, I don't care about anything else and find myself longing to be with my Lord forever.

I know from firsthand experience that God has always been there when I needed Him. He has always come through when I have called to Him for help. Although His timing is different than what I want or expect, He has never let me down. It is because of this that I can trust Him, I know He will be there to the end and through the end unto eternity!

This is what Christianity is all about. This is the theme of the entire Bible. All 66 books were written to explain the plan of God from the beginning. God knew we would need a savior from death. God knew we needed a way to experience life and He provided it. It was prophesied from thousands of years ago that God would send a savior for humankind and He did. He outlined the cost of this sacrifice in the Old Testament stories. If you don't know who you are in Christ, find out! Search the scriptures for what they say about the way God views you.

If you have a Fear of Death let me pray for you now:

Lord, it is hard to grasp that death is just a gateway. It is frightening when we can't see beyond this gate into the eternal. Give us the faith to trust in you and the way you have provided to overcome death and enter eternal life. I pray for those who don't know you and have walked away from the life that you bring. Help them to find you and to get to know you for who you really are.

I pray for anyone experiencing the Fear of Death. I pray for complete deliverance from this fear once and for all. As we turn to you and read your word, help us to understand and experience life. May we be free from the grip of death and come to see the victory that you have achieved over death. In you, we need not fear death anymore. Thank you, Lord, Amen.

I have covered the fears that I see people most frequently struggle with. In all fears, the answer to overcoming is found in the one who has overcome, Jesus Christ. But what if you fear God?

Despite what you may think, no matter how bad you have been, God will not strike you down with lightning if you enter a church or a place of worship. He loves you. If you want to get to know God, there is nothing to fear. If you want to get to know God, just ask and He will help you.

Don't fear what He may ask you to do. Despite many opinions, God does not ask everyone to sell all of their things and move to Africa. If He does, you will be prepared. You will not be doing it out of fear but out of joy.

In the words of God Himself to Jeremiah,
> *"For I know the plans I have for you, plans to prosper you and not to harm you, plans to give you hope and a future." Jeremiah 29:11*

No matter what God asks of you, the reward you will gain will be worth any cost.

Chapter 15
It's not about the Money
Why does the church always ask for money?

"Let no debt remain outstanding, except the continuing debt to love one another..."
Romans 13:8

Are you a person that gets excited about giving? Take a few moments to go through the questions below and honestly think about the impact of money in your life.

How do you respond when a person knocks on your door collecting money for a local charity? Do you hide quietly behind the curtain, hoping they will go away? If you do give, what goes through your mind when deciding how much to give?

What about birthdays and Christmas time, do you give because of an underlying obligation? Do you expect to receive a gift back? When you receive a gift, do you estimate its value so that you may reciprocate accordingly?

What about when the bag comes around in church, what feelings arise?

Does it bring you joy to give to others in need? Do you actively search for ways to give?

We tend to spend far too much time thinking about how to make money that we forget about how we are spending our money. There is so much we can learn about God, ourselves and others from the way we handle our money. What I'm trying to get at, is that I think all of us could learn a few lessons about giving. For most of us, giving doesn't come naturally. It is something we have to work at.

Having been around the church for quite a long time, I have seen some interesting forms of giving, some have absolutely blown me away. I know one particular lady in our church that loves to sew. She gathers donations of beautiful material and then spends day after day sewing beautiful, designer-like outfits for children of all ages. When teams from our church go on mission trips, she sends these clothes with them and blesses children all over the world with designer outfits!

Another family entrusted their entire business to God. As the business grew, they seemingly employed half the church! They use their financial success to bless the members of the church over and over in ways beyond what I could ever imagine giving.

I've seen new mothers, who are still learning to cope with a new baby, gather and do big bake-offs and freeze meals for families in need. They volunteer to watch each other's children so that parents can have some downtime.

There is one man in our church who claims he is retired, yet he built a maintenance shed at the back of the church. In it he stores all the tools he needs to come into church voluntarily, just about every day, to fix anything that needs fixing. He will do any job you ask him to, with such joy and never a complaint!

I've seen anonymous finances being supplied to help those in times of hardship. As I said earlier, I have been blown away by the methods people use to give and I've seen the joy it brings to everyone, including the giver.

But unfortunately, I have also seen another type of giving.

Did you know that the church is probably the biggest second-hand burial ground? It is where the unwanted items of hundreds of people get dumped with the assumption their stuff will somehow bless someone else. Don't get me wrong, I'm sure some those items could bless someone but they could be stored elsewhere until the need is known or the items could just be given to the businesses designed to deal with second-hand goods.

When we ask for donated items to take to an orphanage we sponsor; we have to specify only new items. Otherwise, you would not believe your eyes at what people will drop off. We have often received old, dirty and just downright ugly items. You know that either someone's great-grandma died and left behind these things or they were doing a massive spring-cleaning and didn't want the stuff in their house anymore.

Imagine if we were to take those items to an orphanage. What message does that send to the children about our "Christian" organization? Do you think they would desire to know the God we serve knowing that we live in a very wealthy society by just about anyone's standards and yet we give them the leftovers? Would you feel loved receiving someone else's rubbish?

Have a look sometime at all the unwanted junk that gets left in the church. Most of it has stains, stinks or is falling apart. No one knows where it came from or what to do with it. Believe me, if there is a need, most churches will specifically ask for those particular items.

There is a story from the Bible that always pricks my heart when I am about to give something to the church. It is the story of David's offering to God. David is told to build an altar to the Lord on the threshing floor of a man named Araunah the Jebusite.

> *So David went up, as the Lord had commanded through Gad. When Araunah looked and saw the king and his men coming toward him, he went out and bowed down before the king with his face to the ground.*
>
> *Araunah said, "Why has my lord the king come to his servant?"*

"To buy your threshing floor," David answered, *"so I can build an altar to the Lord, that the plague on the people may be stopped."*

Araunah said to David, "Let my lord the king take whatever pleases him and offer it up. Here are oxen for the burnt offering, and here are threshing sledges and ox yokes for the wood. O king, Araunah gives all this to the king." Araunah also said to him, "May the Lord your God accept you."

But the king replied to Araunah, "No, I insist on paying you for it. I will not sacrifice to the Lord my God burnt offerings that cost me nothing." So David bought the threshing floor and the oxen and paid fifty shekels of silver for them. 2 Samuel 24:19-24

You can throw money to charities and good causes but what does it mean to you? Does your giving ever challenge you?

David refused to give unto God that which cost him nothing. When we are giving to the church or as an act of obedience unto God, we should feel the weight of giving; it shows reverence to God's holiness. Your giving is an act of worship unto the Almighty God.

When people give an offering at church, they should give their best to God, not just what is leftover at the end of the week. Some people show up to church unprepared, empty their pockets and just dump into the offering bag whatever coins are leftover. Those who put God first set aside a portion of their wages at the beginning of the week and purposefully come to church prepared to give to God. If you're going to give, especially when you give as you would unto God, give with intention.

> *On the first day of every week, each one of you should set aside a sum of money in keeping with his income, saving it up, so that when I come no collections will have to be made.*
>
> 1 Corinthians 16:2

Imagine if people came forward each week eager to give what they have saved up ahead of time to God and the church. If Christians were doing the right thing, the church wouldn't need to ask for money. Yet we are human and the fact is, we simply forget, even when we shouldn't. Offering time at church is a prompting for those who belong to a church. If you're not a member, you should feel no obligation to give.

Believe me, most pastors don't enjoy asking for money. Sadly in most churches, if the pastor doesn't remind people to give, the tithes drop off and parts of the church's ministries suffer.

Simply running a church costs money. They have all the same bills we do – electricity, water, phones, heating/air conditioning, people to man the offices, cleaners, etc. The church is a symbolic representation and the first impression many have of God and it should be kept in the same or even better condition than our own homes. Don't you agree?

When I give money to the church, I think of it as one way of giving back to God a portion of what he has blessed me with. I know that our church uses that money to not only run the church but to bless others.

In the community, guess where people often go when they are in need? That's right, the church. The church supplies anything from meals and clothes to gift cards for food and fuel. Again that costs money.

If you are not sure where the church spends its money, ask! Our church is very open about where the money goes. You can attend the AGM each year or ask the front desk and they will give you a copy of the financial statement saying exactly where the money goes.

If someone asking for money offends you, I would challenge you to have a look at your giving patterns. A person asking for money doesn't offend people who are givers. You always have the option to say, "no". No one needs to know how much you give. It's between you and God as to where your money goes.

The leaders of the church are only following what God has laid out clearly in His Word, the Bible. God commands His people to tithe, whether we like it or not.

> *I, the Lord do not change...*

> *Will a man rob God? Yet you rob me. But you ask, 'How do we rob you?'*

> *'In tithes and offerings. You are under a curse- the whole nation of you- because you are robbing me. Bring the whole tithe into the storehouse, that there may be food in my house. Test me in this,' says the Lord Almighty, 'and see if I will not throw open the floodgates of heaven and pour out so much blessing that you will not have room enough for it.'* Malachi 3:6, 8-10

God does everything to grow our faith and this is an exceptional area to do that. Giving a tithe of everything that you earn to the Lord, helps us to keep a healthy perspective of money. It shows that we are in control of the money and are not allowing money to control us. It is a huge commitment of faith to God but one that He generously rewards. When we give something that has cost us some effort and we do it in such a way that doesn't bring attention back to ourselves, there is a secret blessing we receive. It is quite hard to put into words so may I encourage you to give it a try and see for yourself what happens? This is one area that God says to test Him and see for yourself the blessing He will provide.

What I love about the tithe of the Old Testament is that it was a percentage. It was based on ten percent. Even the poor could give ten percent of what they earn and it gave God just as much glory as someone who gave ten percent of a million. Today the amount you give should be prayerfully considered. Ask God to guide you in this manner. The important thing is to just start. Like everything else in the Christian faith, you need to step out and move in faith. If you are already in the habit of tithing, you may, like David, want to give something that challenges you or gives you a pinch of discomfort to challenge your faith.

If you are unable to give anything because you don't have an income, you may look at giving of your time in service to the church. Unfortunately in most churches and community volunteer centers, the statistic tends to be twenty percent of the people do eighty percent of the work. That in itself shows that we need to learn how to give not only of our finances but of ourselves. When we stop giving, we become self-absorbed. Just turn on the news or look around at the state of the world to see the consequences of that self-absorption.

If we could get our head around the art of giving, imagine the difference it would make in our world! People would learn how to share and smile a bit more. We would learn to be content with less and not strive so hard to outdo one another. No one would need to beg for money because his or her needs would be met. It's interesting; God has provided enough abundance in our world, that there should be neither poverty nor starvation anywhere. So where does the real problem reside? It resides in the greediness of mankind.

God even has to go so far as to remind people to take care of their own families!

> *If anyone does not provide for his relatives, and especially for his immediate family, he has denied the faith and is worse than an unbeliever.* 1 Timothy 5:8

Take a moment to contemplate what we are teaching to our children and the generation of kids in our lives. Think about what they observe from us. What do their eyes see? How do they see us respond to the needs around us?

When you go to an amusement park or the local pool, do you lie about their age so they can get in for less money? Do you say they are younger to get a free meal at a restaurant? Think about the message that sends to our kids, that it's okay to lie for money. And speaking of honesty in money matters, how honest are you with your money? Do you report honestly in your income tax review? Do you pay what you should be paying or are you skirting around the truth to avoid spending money?

> *Dishonest money dwindles away, but he who gathers money little by little makes it grow.* Proverbs 13:11

Take a moment to think about what you teach others by the way you manage your money. Maybe it's time to revisit where your money is going, what habits need to change and what needs to be fixed up or reported on official documents. Money can slowly lead us astray and we need to go back and evaluate its effect on our lives.

> *For the love of money is a root of all kinds of evil. Some people, eager for money, have wandered from the faith and pierced themselves with many griefs.* 1 Timothy 6:10

You don't have to look very far to see those who have been lead away from any moral standard to follow the path of fame and fortune. They justify themselves and blame others but deep down they know they are the cause of their own misfortune. Unfortunately, those who compromise who they are for money are often the ones who have a tragic ending. Is the love of money worth losing your soul?

> *Keep your lives free from the love of money and be content with what you have, because God has said, "Never will I leave you; never will I forsake you." Hebrews 13:5*

Being content is the key to happiness. Being grateful for what we do have instead of focusing on what we don't, helps us to put our priorities into perspective. Just check out the latest youtube videos or Netflix shows to see more and more people enjoying the benefits that come from minimalism, de-cluttering and downsizing. Happiness does not come from having more! God doesn't want you to miss out on what life is really about.

God gives us the things in our lives to teach us how to be good stewards of what He has entrusted to us. God does not need your money. He already owns everything. He is the one who supplies all of *our* needs. If you think you are the source of your income be careful for you would be amazed how quickly you can lose everything. We are more dependent upon God than we think.

He wants us to use the money and resources He has blessed us with to bless others. This is to help you more than it helps the people around you. It's a bit like forgiveness in that it frees you from the bondage it can potentially trap you in. If you chase money, you will never have enough. When you buy a bigger house, you need more furniture and it costs more to upkeep. When you buy a lifestyle you have to pay dearly to keep it up. More stuff means more time looking after more stuff. Working more means less time with family and friends. Then when you acquire much, who is to say what can happen? In a moment, you could lose everything you ever worked for.

Money is a no-win game; it's just another mirage. No matter how much you acquire, in the end, you can't take it with you and it will go to someone else. All of your wealth will be passed on and you will have no control over what someone else does with it. King Solomon was known to be the wisest man that ever lived. He wrote the following passage around 935 BC.

> *Whoever loves money never has money enough; whoever loves wealth is never satisfied with his income. This too is meaningless. As goods increase, so do those who consume them. And what benefit are they to the owner except to feast his eyes on them?*
>
> *The sleep of a laborer is sweet whether he eats little or much, but the abundance of a rich man permits him no sleep.*
>
> *I have seen a grievous evil under the sun: wealth hoarded to the harm of its owner, or wealth lost through some misfortune, so that when he has a son there is nothing left for him.*
>
> *Naked a man comes from his mother's womb, and as he comes, so he departs. He takes nothing from his labor that he can carry in his hand.   Ecclesiastes 5:10-15*

Jesus also taught people the truth about money. He tried to convey the message of how important it is to invest in others rather than in material items. He knew how easily we lose focus of what is really important in life. Read what He spoke to the people of his generation in 29 AD.

> *Do not store up for yourselves treasures on earth, where moth and rust destroy, and where thieves break in and steal. But store up for yourselves treasures in heaven, where moth and rust do not*

destroy, and where thieves do not break in and steal. For where your treasure is, there your heart will be also.

The eye is the lamp of the body. If your eyes are good, your whole body will be full of light. But if your eyes are bad, your whole body will be full of darkness. If then the light within you is darkness, how great is that darkness!

No one can serve two masters. Either he will hate the one and love the other, or he will be devoted to the one and despise the other. You cannot serve both God and Money. Matthew 6:19-24

When you read this passage you may question why the second paragraph is there. It seems to not relate, yet the eyes are often the source where our money trouble stems from. Often we enter the deadly comparison game and we see the things someone else has and want to buy them for ourselves. We all have done this at some point.

I used to admire my friends' beautiful houses when mine seemed like a dump with toys, clothes and a random assortment of mess everywhere. As I brought my frustration to God, He showed me how to be content with what I had and to enjoy my life. I began to genuinely be happy for my friends and would enjoy visiting them more often. Their friendship meant more than anything that I could own and their beautiful houses blessed me too! I found that going to their house would refresh me like a visit to a day spa.

We also fall prey to the media. Advertising is a big industry for a reason- it works! I know in my house I had to put up a sign saying, "No Junk Mail" because our whole family would look at those weekly magazines and always see something that we would "need". If you're not looking, you won't know what you're 'missing out' on.

Many people link power and control to having money, but notice that Jesus said, "You cannot serve both God and money." No one can serve two masters and there will always be a "master" in your life. You have to make a choice. You may think you are the "master" of your life. You can do everything possible to try and control your life and then be hit by disaster or disease tomorrow. You do not have control. When you realize this, you have gained much wisdom. Choose wisely to whom or what you will serve.

Do notice, however, that you can serve God and have money. You can also serve God and use money. I point this out because there is no sin in being wealthy. Despite many people's perceived notions of Jesus, He was not poor. No one knows exactly how much He had but it is recorded in one instance that Judas had an issue with Mary pouring expensive perfume on the feet of Jesus and he spoke against her wastefulness.

> *He did not say this because he cared about the poor but because he was a thief; as keeper of the money bag, he used to help himself to what was put into it.* John 12:6

For someone to regularly steal from a moneybag, there has to be something in it. It's not talked about much because Jesus had no concern for money. It was a tool used to get to where He needed to be. Jesus held a proper perspective of money. It was not a snare for Him, although sadly it was a snare for His disciple, Judas. As I said before, when you compromise your integrity for money, often there is a tragic end. Judas ended up hanging himself from the guilt of being controlled by money.

Giving is a heart attitude and as we have already discussed, God is interested in the heart behind your giving.

> *Give generously to them and do so without a grudging heart; then because of this the Lord your God will bless you in all your work and in everything you put your hand to. There will always be*

> *poor people in the land. Therefore I command you to be openhanded toward your brothers and toward the poor and needy in your land.* Deuteronomy 15:10-11.

As Christians, we are to be ambassadors for Christ, representing Him in our words and our actions. One day we will be held to account for what we have given with our time, our talents, and our money. How would you sum up what you have done with what you have been given? Are you under the control of money? Where is your treasure?

Look at where you spend most of your time and your money; this is a good measure of where your treasure truly is. Map out where you spend your time and your money on a piece of paper. Ask God if you need to make some changes.

Examine your job. Are you working just to make money or is your work a place to take the time to value others? Our jobs, whether we are paid or not, should bring about satisfaction in our lives. If they are not, we need to ask God if we should change jobs. Sometimes we may be in the right job but need a change of heart on how we view our job. Let God into your working life. Let Him guide you to where you are meant to be.

Take a look at your personal life. Ask your loved ones if they feel you treasure them. What adjustments do you need to make to let your spouse or your children know that you value them and love to spend time with them? Make the time to reinvest in your friendships.

> *For where your treasure is, there your heart will also be.*
> Matthew 6:21

The way you live your life is a witness to everyone around you showing what is important to you. What are you saying by the way you live your life?

Chapter 16
Can I get a Witness?
Do I have to be a door knocker?

And you will be my witnesses... to the ends of the earth.
Acts 1:8

If you know a Christian or are a Christian, I'm sure at some point, you have felt the pressure and the intimidating feeling of being a "witness" or being "witnessed" to. It can be quite an awkward situation and it can be very uncomfortable or embarrassing.

Witnessing is a big and fancy word for just sharing what God is doing in your life. It is not meant to be a sales job. Whatever you believe about God, it is not your place to shove your opinions of God down someone else's throat. God simply asks that we love others and give glory to Him. If people ask us questions, we are to be prepared with an answer.

> *But in your hearts set apart Christ as Lord. Always be prepared to give an answer to everyone who asks you to give the reason for the hope that you have. But do this with gentleness and respect, keeping a clear conscience, so that those who speak maliciously against your good behavior in Christ may be ashamed of their slander.* 1 Peter 3:15-16

Let's get something straight right upfront, if you have accepted Jesus Christ as Lord of your life and are in a relationship with him, you are already a witness to those around you. As others discover that there is something different about you because you are a Christian, the art of witnessing is on! You are either a good ambassador for Christ or you misrepresent what Jesus is about and if we truthfully look into our lives, we will realize that we have all been or done a bit of both. The more time we spend drawing closer to Jesus (worshiping God, praying, reading the Scripture, fellowshipping with our family in Christ, waiting upon the Lord for revelation and obeying what He directs us to do) the better the witness we will be.

Share your story.

Before I became a Christian, I spent years in overwhelming sadness that I didn't understand the purpose of life. I just existed and got through each day (and there were a lot of hard days!) No one understood what was going on in my heart and soul. I tried to talk to others about it and they could relate to my pain, but they didn't have answers either! I walked around without a vision or purpose for my life. I was always wondering what was I meant to do with my life?

Then I met someone who had joy and a smile on her face. She was so kind to me, unlike anyone I had met before. As we became friends, we would walk together just about every night for "exercise" and we had some amazing conversations. She listened to my stories and told me about how she had found joy in her life. She patiently answered hundreds of questions I had about the Bible and God. And any answers she didn't know, she would say, "I'll get back to you about that one" or "Give me some time to see if I can find that answer for you".

She then invited me along to church to find out the answers for myself. And the very first time I went to her church, it was like the preacher was talking to just me! At the end of his message, he asked if anyone wanted to come forward and give their heart to the Lord. I was frozen in my seat but my friend looked at me, saw what I wanted to do and said, "Come on, let's go" and went with me to talk to the pastor. I thank God for that little nudge! When I got to the front and accepted Jesus as my Savior, Lord of my life, the tears that had been built up over the years of sadness started to fall. I wept and wept, and went through an entire tissue box. I couldn't help it; they just kept falling. As every tear fell, I felt more and more sadness being lifted from my soul. Absolute joy overflowed in my heart that what I had been searching for was now mine! I felt lighter and cleaner and exhausted! It took so much out of me that when people from the church were talking to me afterward, I was too drained to answer anything but "yes" or "no". They seemed to understand.

I was so excited about this joy that I found that I wanted to tell my friends and family about it. When I went to tell them that I had met my Creator and asked him to be Lord of my life, I didn't receive the excited response that I had expected. Instead of people being happy for me, they made fun of me or looked at me with that "You poor misled child" look. I wondered what was wrong with these people? Why weren't they as excited as I was about Jesus?

Granted, I was probably a bit overwhelming in my enthusiasm to share Jesus with others, but I didn't expect such a negative response. Something in me told me to be quiet about my newfound knowledge. I became awkward about telling others about Jesus and slowly became shy and embarrassed by my Christianity. This was compounded by one particular person who loved to see me mess up and then would say, "Oh, is that what a Christian is supposed to be like?" It made for a rough start to my Christian journey. It was hard to let Jesus shine when I was so self-conscious and awkward.

As I began to grow as a young Christian, I listened to other Christians telling me about how they had led people to know the Lord. They seemed so confident in their faith. I watched great evangelists like Billy Graham simply speak and thousands of people would repent and accept Jesus as their Lord. I felt sadly lacking.

I went to a couple of seminars and classes on witnessing and received "fail-proof" techniques in witnessing that still didn't seem to work for me. They just didn't feel natural but very "put on" or fake. Many of the things I learned I didn't even try. Then I would carry around guilt for not being bold enough for Christ, along with the only verse that seemed to stick in my mind from my witnessing courses:

> *If anyone is ashamed of me and my words, the Son of Man will be ashamed of him when he comes in his glory and in the glory of the Father and of the holy angels.*   Luke 9:26

Be yourself.

Over time I realized I wasn't ashamed of Christ, I was ashamed to present him in the ways that I was taught. I didn't feel comfortable with a 5 step method to tell someone about a relationship with God.

The problem with using other people's techniques for witnessing is that those techniques are what worked for them and will not necessarily work the same way for you. God wants you and me to witness to others in the way He designed us to witness. There is no "right" way to witness. After all, to be a "witness" to others is not something that you struggle to DO; it's who you are! It is Christ, who dwells within you working his way out through your unique character and design. We are each unique creations in the Lord and the way you witness is designed to reach those people the Lord puts into your life. It brings joy to God as he watches the variety and contrast between His children in the way that they share Jesus (His Son) to others.

When you try to act like another Christian, no matter how great they are, you will look silly because it is like putting on clothes that are not your own. Certainly, take advice and learn from the wisdom of others but don't pick up things that are not yours to take. Don't compare yourself to what someone else is successfully doing. This is not only important in witnessing but in every area of your life. Live the life that God has called you to live and don't look to others for their approval or opinion and stop the comparison game!

It's like the story of David I touched upon earlier. David feels God has called him to defeat the giant who was intimidating the army of Israel. Saul, the King, tries to convince David to fight the giant, using his own "tried and true" battle techniques. David listens and even tries on Saul's armor, but then decides it would be better to go into battle as himself.

> Then Saul dressed David in his own tunic. He put a coat of armor on him and a bronze helmet on his head. David fastened on his sword over the tunic and tried walking around, because he was not used to them.
>
> "I cannot go in these," he said to Saul, "because I am not used to them." So he took them off. Then he took his staff in his hand, chose five smooth stones from the stream, put them in the pouch of his shepherd's bag and, with his sling in his hand, approached the Philistine.
>
> David said to the Philistine, "You come against me with sword and spear and javelin, but I come against you in the name of the LORD Almighty, the God of the armies of Israel, whom you have defied.
>
> All those gathered here will know that it is not by sword or spear that the LORD saves; for the battle is the LORD's, and he will give all of you into our hands."
>
> As the Philistine moved closer to attack him, David ran quickly toward the battle line to meet him. Reaching into his bag and taking out a stone, he slung it and struck the Philistine on the forehead. The stone sank into his forehead, and he fell facedown on the ground.
>
> So David triumphed over the Philistine with a sling and a stone; without a sword in his hand he struck down the Philistine and killed him.   1 Samuel 17:38-40, 45, 47-50

David was triumphant in defeating Goliath because he didn't listen to what others were saying around him but relied on his faith in God. He used the skills given to him by God, the skills he was comfortable with (a slingshot and some stones, perfect for a boy his age) and defeated the giant. Had he tried to fight this battle with someone else's armor, I don't think he would have had the victory and it would have been a different story altogether.

We are in a battle too.

> *Our struggle is not against flesh and blood, but against the rulers, against the authorities, against the powers of this dark world and against the spiritual forces of evil in the heavenly realms. Ephesians 6:12*

This is a battle over people's eternal lives in the spiritual realm. We have to rely on what God directs us to do because only He can see into the spiritual realm of other people's lives. So using simple methods or techniques taught to us by man, cannot fully reach into someone's life like following God's direction. Only God knows what another person will be receptive to on that particular day in time.

Trying to imitate another person in witnessing is also a very dangerous practice because we are not being completely truthful about our own experience of Christ in our lives.

> *A truthful witness does not deceive, but a false witness pours out lies. Proverbs 14:5*

> *A truthful witness saves lives, but a false witness is deceitful. Proverbs 14:25*

I realized that the guidelines and tracts I picked up were what other people put together and it was their witness, not mine. When we witness, we must speak the truth, not making up anything. Don't exaggerate. Be honest about what Christ has done in your life and what that means to you.

> *I desire to do your will, O my God; your law is within my heart. I proclaim righteousness (your saving acts) in the great assembly; I do not seal my lips, Lord, as you know, O Lord. I do not hide your righteousness in my heart; I speak of your faithfulness and salvation. I do not conceal your love and your truth from the great assembly.* Psalm 40:8-10

Speak about God regularly.

Before we focus on a world that does not know Christ, I wonder how often we speak of God and His works of righteousness in our lives to those who already know Christ? Do we speak of Christ with our Christian friends and family members?

> *Teach them to your children, talking about them when you sit at home and when you walk along the road, when you lie down and when you get up.* Deuteronomy 11:19

I don't often have a great assembly of people around me, but one place I do is when I go to church. I think it is important to declare the goodness of God to other people around me at church.

This is so important for many reasons. First, believe it or not, not everyone in the church is in a relationship with Jesus. Many people can talk the talk without actually knowing Jesus personally.

If you are in any healthy, growing church, you will also have new people coming into church every week who don't know God yet. It is important to share with them the great things God has done in your life. By speaking frequently of God's goodness, it changes conversations in the right direction. If we do not season our conversation with the salt of God, conversations can quickly turn towards sarcasm, gossip or other inappropriate sharing.

Continually speaking about God and what He's currently doing in our lives, encourages others around us in the struggles they may be going through.

All of us have phases of our lives where we just need to hear that God is still alive and working all things to His purpose. The testimonies of others build us up and encourage us to keep going.

Speaking to others in the church is just good practice. By sharing frequently about God in a place where we feel comfortable, we speak more naturally when we are with non-Christians or in the workplace. This is because we are already used to speaking about God and it is no longer awkward.

Study the Bible.

The one good thing that I have picked up from others concerning our witness to others is that we all should know what salvation means, how a person can be sure of their salvation and scriptures to back up your answers.

I would encourage you, if you haven't already, to take the time to look up the passages in the Bible that talk about salvation. How do you know that you are saved? What does the Bible say about salvation? Can you earn your salvation? Can you lose your salvation?

Study the book of Romans. Look up the meaning of the words that define salvation: righteousness, justification, sanctification and glorification. Look up the Bible verses that speak about salvation and ask God to teach you about them. Memorize these scriptures and meditate on them to gain understanding, so they are familiar to you and become part of your story. Here are a few to get you started:

> *For God so loved the world that he gave his one and only Son, that whoever believes in him shall not perish but have eternal life. For God did not send his Son into the world to*

condemn the world, but to save the world through him.   John 3:16-17

If you declare with your mouth, "Jesus is Lord," and believe in your heart that God raised him from the dead, you will be saved. For it is with your heart that you believe and are justified, and it is with your mouth that you profess your faith and are saved.   Romans 10:9-10

When the disciples heard this, they were greatly astonished and asked, "Who then can be saved?" Jesus looked at them and said, "With man this is impossible, but with God all things are possible."   Matthew 19: 25-26

How do you learn more about Jesus and what He has done? Read, search and study the Bible. Don't be a lazy Christian, expecting others to teach you all of the time. They may not be teaching you correctly. But how would you know unless you search the scriptures for yourself? Start each day by looking up the scriptures and know what they say.

If you haven't had the time to explore scripture and the opportunity arises to talk about Jesus, don't let the lack of Biblical knowledge stop you. Simply share what Christ has done in your life and how you felt about that.

Allow the Holy Spirit to guide you.
Remember, it's not your job to change a person. It's God's job to change a person's heart. You cannot lead a person to trust in Christ on your own. Only God and the Holy Spirit moving through you can prepare one's heart to accept Jesus as Lord and Savior. It is God who gives the prompting and strength that a person needs to accept this call. To assume that we can do anything for God successfully apart from God guiding us is just silly. When Christ moves through us and we are obedient to do or say what He has

prompted, then we can rest knowing that we have done enough, no matter what the response is.

Pray.

If God has brought a particular person to mind to share the message of hope in Christ, then the very first thing you should do is begin to pray! Everything you attempt to do for God should begin with prayer. Prayer makes sure you are on the right track, covers you and the people around you, and is a faithful reminder that you are dependent on God.

When people around you are suffering, take their burdens before the Lord and ask Him to use those burdens to lead them into a relationship with Jesus. Pray that God will use you to encourage them. Prayer is a powerful and effective weapon that God has given to us as Christians.

Have you ever set aside time specifically to pray for someone? Set aside an entire hour to pray for someone. You will be amazed at what you receive from this experience. As you pray for that person, maybe you could write a letter of encouragement to them. Include any verses that let that person know they are loved by God. Can you imagine how good you would feel if someone gave you that kind of letter? Just knowing that someone has taken time out of his or her busy schedule to pray for you is powerful. Who in this day and age cares that much?

I remember when I taught high school classes, I would take the list of students and pray over every boy or girl who would be in my class for the upcoming year. This not only covered them in prayer but also gave me the insight to know what I should be expecting from each student. It prepared me in ways only God could. As the year progressed and as opportunities would arise, I would let students know that I had been praying for them. I remember pulling aside one particularly difficult student and letting him know that I had been praying for him to do well in class and in other areas he was struggling with, and the reaction from his face was priceless. He was speechless. Later in the year, he thanked me for praying for him and asked me to continue to do so.

Make a list of people in your workplace or your life and begin to pray for them each day.

If someone is struggling, often I will take the person aside and ask, "Can I pray for you?" I rarely have anyone answer "no," but if they do, I simply respect their request. Sometimes I may ask is there anything else I can do for you? But at least they know in the future who to look for if they do want some prayer.

I can't stress this enough: If you say you are going to pray for someone, mean it! Don't say you're going to pray and then not do it. Too often "I'll pray for you" is just a glib phrase we use to get out of a situation that we don't want to be in. I've been guilty of this in the past. I didn't know how to respond so I'd tell the person I would pray and then I'd leave. The Holy Spirit challenged my hypocritical spirit on this. Now if I see someone in pain or struggling, I stop right there and then and pray for the person. By doing so, I prioritize the person and it helps me to remember to continue praying for them.

Once you have prayed, be open to opportunities!

> *And if you greet only your own people, what are you doing more than others? Do not even pagans do that?* Matthew 5:47

Get out of your comfort zone.
There are so many new people who come into church only to walk back out again because no one takes the time to greet and meet them. The Christians are all busy catching up with their friends. And I know what that is like, sometimes Sunday feels like the only time to catch up with everyone. But Jesus said, "Go and make disciples", not "Go catch up with your friends." And you never know, you might be missing out on the most amazing friendship

yet. Why not make it a point to find someone new to invite over to your circle of friends?

You don't need to go on a mission trip when the mission is coming to you. This is the easiest evangelism ever! The new people who grace the door of your church are already interested. They wouldn't be there if they weren't. They want to get to know new people. They want to learn what your church is like. They want to hear your story. Jump in and get to know someone.

A witness is one who has seen, heard or learned about Jesus. A witness is not Jesus, but one who has experienced Jesus. You do not have to be a minister, preacher or evangelist. You don't need to be "qualified" in any way to be a witness. It is better that you are not "qualified", then you will rely more on Christ than on what you have been taught by man.

Live as a representative of Christ Jesus.

Just being a Christian is a witness to others. So much is learned about a person by observing their life. What is being displayed in your Christian walk? How do you react to the world around you?

Love not only your friends but also your enemies. Pray for them because if God gets hold of them, He can change them. He will do it more powerfully, effectively and quickly than you ever could. Instead of getting offended and angry, understand that most people do not have an understanding of God and His word. How can they be held accountable for things that they have never seen nor heard?

> *He himself was not the light; he came only as a witness to the light. The true light that gives light to every man was coming into the world.* John 1:8

Even John the Baptist, as great a man as he was, came only to be a witness to Jesus. He did that by just being who God designed him to be. That is all that God asks of us. God has given us everything we need to be His representative in this world and to live life the way it was designed to be lived.

He has even given us spiritual armor to wear each day as we go into the battles of this world.

Put on Spiritual Armor
Ephesians 6:10-18

We can wear a spiritual armor that God has designed personally for each of us.

> *Therefore put on the full armor of God, so that when the day of evil comes, you may be able to stand your ground, and after you have done everything, to stand. Ephesians 6:13*

The Belt of Truth – You need to have the courage to hear the truth, the boldness to face the truth in your own life and the confidence to speak the truth. The truth is what brings freedom to your life. In God, you will find the real truth and it will set you free. (John 8:32) When truth reigns in your life, you are no longer deceived by the lies people tell and what the world may teach you. You begin to see things as they are. It is the truth that brings you to the realization that God does love you. The truth tells you who you are in Christ- loved, cherished and protected. It is the truth that leads you to know God through Jesus Christ. It is the truth that will be a vital part of your armor in your battles. As a belt holds up the rest of the armor, the truth holds up the rest of your spiritual armor.

Breastplate of Righteousness – This is God's righteousness, not yours; yet we wear it as our own because of what He has done. You can't gain the victory that God will give without placing Him first and foremost in your life. He needs to be in the command center of your life. When you accept Jesus as Lord, He is the breastplate of armor. He protects the vital organs keeping you alive. He keeps your heart warm and tender, not cold, numb and rock hard. Nothing is gained without this very important piece of armor.

Feet Fitted with Readiness (that comes from the gospel of peace) – Knowing the truth is great, but you don't go anywhere until you step out in that truth. You need to be ready to obey and to do what God is calling you to do. It is time to get off that well-warmed church seat and start living a proactive, God-led life. Are you ready to have a relationship with your Creator? Are you ready to walk out your faith?

Are you ready to actively love, looking for ways to bring peace into people's lives? Through the Spirit of God, we have peace within us that will steady us in any storm. Yet everywhere we walk, we bring that peace with us and can share it with those around us. Instead of reacting, we can respond by bringing calm to the rough seas of life. We leave footprints of peace wherever we go.

Shield of Faith – Even when we can't see the light at the end of the tunnel, it is our faith that says it is there and if we are patient, we will see it soon. Faith is a choice we have to make. We have to pick it up and hold it like a shield. We can't let go of it or we become more vulnerable in the battle.

Faith is a lot like love. So many people think love is based on a feeling or emotion. But those who are celebrating silver and golden wedding anniversaries will tell you that love is a choice. If you based love on emotion or feelings, you'd never survive a long healthy marriage. Love is a commitment. You decide that you will love a person, no matter what you may feel. It is the same with faith. You decide that you will love and follow God, no matter what you feel, even if you can't see Him.

> *Now faith is being sure of what we hope for and certain of what we do not see.* Hebrews 11:1

(Hebrews Chapter 11 is all about amazing examples of faith throughout time.)

Helmet of Salvation – This is a critical piece of armor. It protects your mind, the place where the battles begin and end. Jesus has given us salvation yet we need to discover how we can respond. We can find out everyday by reading the word He has given us. Trust me, you could read through the Bible every day for the rest of your life and never truly understand all that God has done for you. But we need to try. We have to get it into our brains. We need to memorize His word, meditate on it and pray it. We have to know that Jesus Christ has saved us. When we know this, it protects us from the doubts that will continually come. It will overcome the lies spoken to us and the deceptions so easily believed. We need to remind ourselves daily who we are in Jesus Christ so we protect our thoughts from wandering.

The Sword of the Spirit – This is the only offensive weapon that we have in the spiritual realm and it is two-fold.

The sword is the word of God (the Bible) owned and operated by the Holy Spirit guiding us how and when to use the sword.

The word of God cuts between truth and deception.

> *For the word of God is alive and active. Sharper than any double-edged sword, it penetrates even to dividing soul and spirit, joints and marrow; it judges the thoughts and attitudes of the heart.*
> *Hebrews 4:12*

This is what Jesus himself used to overcome Satan in all of His battles. (Matthew 4) Even when it looked like Satan was winning and Jesus was hanging on the cross, He spoke the word of God. (Matthew 27:46, Psalm 22:1) The word of God is powerful. God spoke creation into being by a word. His words lead to life.

As the Spirit leads us, we need to follow the promptings He places in our hearts. If the Spirit leads you to show love to someone, then do it. Learn to be still and listen to God's promptings through the Holy Spirit.

I like to add the following to the armor that God has given to us:

> *A Crown of Beauty instead of Ashes, The Oil of Gladness instead of Mourning and A Garment of Praise instead of a Spirit of Despair... Isaiah 61:3*

Hey, just because we are in a battle doesn't mean we have to be miserable with an ugly attitude! We are not without hope. God has an amazing ability to bring beauty out of even the most war-torn veterans. We can allow God to bring life into our weary bodies and give us a beauty that goes beyond our suffering and pain. This is how He shines in us and we become light unto the world. We can smile and enjoy our lives!

Conclusion

God does not promise an easy walk. He calls us to a marathon and to finish the race He sets out before us. The good news is whatever He calls us to do, He equips us to do.

Have you ever run a race? I once did a season of cross country running. I don't know how I made it onto the team. I didn't even like running! For me, the hardest part was the first step. But once I started, I developed momentum. Yes, it was still work but I got better at it and as I improved, I actually started to enjoy what I was doing.

As a runner, there are a lot of hard things to overcome. There is training and a change in lifestyle to adapt to being the best runner you can be. Then there's the actual running, one step in front of the other. It doesn't always feel nice. Ask any runner. The shin splints, the "hitting-the-wall" experiences and just the hard slog of it all, yet there is something that rises up in the soul when we attempt to do what we never imagined we could do. And when we actually accomplish what we set out to do, to cross the finish line, we experience a joy that just cannot be put into words. Imagine the day that you cross the finish line into eternity!

Want to catch a glimpse?

Ask any mother who has endured nine long months and very hard labor.

Ask a couple celebrating 50 years of marriage.

Ask a person who has obtained a university degree.

Ask anyone who has finished a race.

With God, things are never easy but we learn so much along the way and He promises to be right there with us the whole way.

Which of the fruit of the Spirit can you develop overnight?

> *The fruit of the Spirit is love, joy, peace, forbearance, kindness, goodness, faithfulness, gentleness and self-control. Against such things there is no law.* Galatians 5:22-23

Love, joy, peace, patience, kindness, goodness, faithfulness, gentleness or self-control? It takes a lifetime to develop any one of them. Yet are they worth developing, you bet! In a culture where everything is fast and furious, I know this is difficult but God is not in a hurry. His timing is perfect. We can rest in the knowledge that He is working and developing our spiritual character each day. As we rest in the knowledge that we are secure in Christ and are open to all He is doing to mature us, we can encourage others.

How can we encourage future generations?

> By coming to God each day seeking His will for the way we speak and act and praying for the people in our lives.
>
> By living out our faith and setting a good example.
>
> By encouraging others rather than judging them, understanding that God calls each of us to a unique journey that only He can lead.
>
> By speaking words of encouragement and mentoring others.
>
> Loving and challenging ourselves and those around us to be better.
>
> Spending time with people and getting involved in their lives in a positive, helpful way.

As a church, we have something powerful to offer to a dying world.

> *Enter through the narrow gate. For wide is the gate and broad is the road that leads to destruction, and many enter through it. But small is the gate and narrow the road that leads to life, and only a few find it.   Matthew 7:13-14*

The road that leads to life, true life, is narrow yet God's greatest desire is to lead us to it. He wants to bless you with life. Not just breathing but a life so beautifully beyond all that we could ask or imagine!

I hope this book encourages you to let go of some of the preconceived ideas you might have held against God and the Christian faith, especially if you are just learning about God or have been hurt by someone in the church. As Christians, I know that we as the "church" can be the guilty party for the cause of such preconceived ideas in others. Yet if you take a closer look, you will begin to see God doing something new within us. As He does, my prayer is that the world around us will be blessed and challenged to do the same.

Discussion Questions

This is your personal private study. If you are using this in a group situation, please answer freely to God and only share in the group what you feel comfortable sharing. Even if you don't share your answers with anyone, take the time to write your answers out so that you can see them clearly and present them to God.

Before we begin this study, list the things or the thoughts that often stop you from coming to God?

What do you hold back from God?

Is there anything you feel you're just not ready to deal with?

Pray that God will help you in all of these things as you answer the study questions for each chapter. Allow God to show you His answers for your life.

Faith Test
Chapter 1 – The Battle
Questions

Questions to answer **before** you read:

What are some of the crazy things going on in your life at the moment?

What are some deeper issues happening in your life at the moment? What are some of the personal battles you are fighting?

What are some of the worst things you or your loved ones have experienced?

When we talk about suffering, which stories from the Bible come to your mind?

How much power do you think satan has?

Please read Chapter One

1. What suffering did Job go through?

2. What have you learned about satan and all angels?

3. What are some things you have learned about suffering?

4. How could suffering be used in a good way?

5. Have you ever had an experience where suffering actually brought you something you needed?

6. What specifically have you learned from your times of suffering?

7. How could you specifically help someone else going through a time of suffering?

Memory verse:
And we know that in all things God works for the good of those who love him, who have been called according to his purpose.   Romans 8:28

Still want a bit more?

Find 3 Bible Verses that deal with suffering and write them below.

Take up the Challenge: Go and do what you answered for number 12.

Faith Test
Chapter 2- Cloudy Days
Questions

Questions to answer **before** you read:

From some of the situations currently happening in your life that you listed from the last chapter, list some possibilities of the good that could arise from that situation.

What was God's ultimate goal in sending His son, Jesus?

Please read Chapter Two

1. What is the difference between suffering and discipline? Pain and maturity?

2. What is the nature of God?

3. What is the character of satan?

4. Define discipline:

5. Describe how a surgeon uses affliction to heal.

6. Describe how God uses affliction to heal.

7. What is the difference between affliction and oppression?

8. I shared how I love the quotation, "Have you ever wanted to ask God why He allows poverty and hunger to exist when He could do something about it? What if He asks you the same question?" What is a favorite quotation you have? Find a couple of new favorites.

9. List as many characteristics of God that you can find in the Bible. (Hint: using a Concordance, Google or a Bible app will make this a lot quicker: search God's character)

Memory Verse:

For he does not willingly bring affliction or grief to the children of men. Lamentations 3:33

Still want a bit more?

Look up Bible verses that show where God allowed or used affliction to discipline someone. (Here's a few to get you started: 2 Chronicles 26:19-20, Daniel 4, Acts 12:21-23, John 9:1-3)

Faith Test
Chapter 3- Becoming a Warrior
Questions

Questions to answer **before** you read:

When you are going through a struggle in your life, what are your coping mechanisms? What things do you find comfort in?

Have you ever experienced struggles that seemingly have always been there and you doubt that they may ever go away?

What are some things that you have tried but definitely have not worked at helping you in a time of trouble?

Please read Chapter Three

1. What is a stronghold?

2. When we turn to the Lord as our place of refuge, why is it the perfect stronghold?

3. How do you perceive life when you are going through hardships?

4. What are some truths about your life that will never change?

5. What is conditional for us to experience God's stronghold in a time of trouble?

6. List the 5 steps of knowing God's will when we face a battle?

      1.
      2.
      3.
      4.
      5.

7. Why is the last step so important?

8. Have you ever felt like God was asking you to do something that was a bit unusual?

9. What happened to David when he obeyed the unusual orders that God gave him?

10. God will never ask you to do what?

Memory Verse:

The Lord is a refuge for the oppressed, a stronghold in times of trouble. Psalm 9:9

Still want a bit more?

Write a prayer to God. Tell Him what's on your mind and ask Him to help you. He's always waiting to hear from you and loves you beyond what you could ever ask or imagine.

Faith Test
Chapter 4- The Warrior Within
Questions

As these chapters begin to get more and more personal, answer the questions for yourself but please do not feel that you need to share any of these answers within the group setting.

Questions to answer **before** you read:

What areas have you struggled to control in your life? (This could be anything from an attitude to a chocolate addiction)

What is it that seems to have its grip within you and that although you may shake it for a while it never fully seems to let go?

What have you tried to loosen its grip on you? What has worked and what hasn't?

Please read Chapter Four

1. What sort of advice have you received in the past when you have shared your struggles with other people?

Good advice:

Bad advice:

2. In your own words, try and summarize what Paul was saying in Romans 7:15-24.

3. How does Revelation 19:11 describe Christ the Messiah?

4. What does a soldier have to do before fighting a battle?

5. Why doesn't God train you to fight in the midst of your battle?

6. Think about the battles you are currently experiencing. What are the specific issues behind the battle? Ask God to show you what other areas of your life He might be training you in areas of obedience?

7. Have you ever stepped out in faith to do something you felt God led you to do? What happened?

8. Have you had times where you felt God was telling you to simply wait? Explain.

9. Think of the issues behind your struggles (ex. Obedience, Complacency, Deception, etc.) Write them out and look up Bible verses that relate to these issues.

Memory Verse:

You armed me with strength for the battle.   Psalm 18:39a

Still want a bit more?

Make time this week to simply sit and be still for an hour. Ask God to speak to you during this time.

Faith Test
Chapter 5- The State of the Heart
Questions

Questions to answer **before** you read:

Can you ever remember a time when you experienced God in a real way? Describe.

If you did a survey of friends and family, would they say you are open to learning new things or stuck in your ways?

What is something new you have learned recently?

Please read Chapter Five

1. According to 1 Samuel 16:7, God looks not at outward appearance but at the heart. Explain what this means.

2. What do you think God is looking for in your heart?

3. Describe the 2 types of heart conditions listed in this chapter.

4. What mistakes have you made recently?

5. What would you say are your weaknesses?

6. How do we make (and keep) our hearts pliable?

7. If you haven't already, read the little book entitled, "My Heart, Christ's Home" by Robert Boyd Munger, InterVarsity Press.

8. True or False. Jesus came into the world to get rid of suffering.

9. Describe the heart.

10. What image are you trying to present in your life?

Memory Verse:

They are darkened in their understanding and separated from the life of God because of the ignorance that is in them due to the hardening of their hearts. Ephesians 4:18

Still want a bit more?

Research what the heart meant to the Jews in Biblical times.

Faith Test
Chapter 6 - Covenant or Contract
Questions

Questions to answer **before** you read:

Have you ever made a contract with someone? Has anyone ever broken a contract with you?

If you made a contract with God, what would you include?

Why did God create so many laws in the Bible?

Please read Chapter 6

1. Describe the similarities between contracts and covenants.

2. Describe the differences between contracts and covenants.

3. Give an example of the unstated laws that humans create.

4. Why does God take His laws seriously and expect us to follow his laws?

5. Are we able to keep the laws set by God?

6. How did Jesus sum up all of the laws?

7. What is more important to God than all of the laws put together?

8. What is faith?

9. Why does faith sometimes seem so distant and impossible to have?

10. Describe another person in the Bible that had faith and yet stumbled occasionally.

Memory Verse:

Fix these words of mine in your hearts and minds; tie them as symbols on your hands and bind them on your foreheads. Teach them to your children, talking about them when you sit at home and when you walk along the road, when you lie down and when you get up.   Deuteronomy 11:18

Still want a bit more?

Begin to write down the ways God has been faithful to you.

Faith Test
Chapter 7- Covenants of the Bible
Questions

Questions to answer **before** you read:

What is one of your most favorite stories?

What do you think the criteria was to have something written about in the Bible?

Please read Chapter 7.

1. What do we need to know in order to have a covenant with God?

2. What was the covenant that God made with Noah?

3. Did it come to pass as God said it would? What doubts do you think Noah had before he saw God establish that covenant?

4. What if God asked you to build an ark. What would be going through your mind?

5. See if you can find two other examples of the flood story in a different cultural aspect.

6. What was the covenant God made with Abraham?

7. What doubts did Abraham have before he saw God establish His covenant? When did Abraham see the evidence of God's covenant?

8. What was God's covenant with Phinehas? Why did God 1 establish this covenant?

9. What was God's covenant with David? What doubts do you think David had before he saw God's covenant established?

10. What covenant has God established with us?

11. What does God ask from us in this covenant?

Explain the Trinity. What does the Holy Spirit do?

Memory Verse:

Jesus replied, "If anyone loves me, he will obey my teaching. My Father will love him, and we will come to him and make our home with him. John 14:23

Still want a bit more?

Write or tell someone the story of your covenant with God so far.

Faith Test
Chapter 8- Hearing from God
Questions

Questions to answer **before** you read:

What are some examples of little things that happen in life that can break your spirit?

What do you do when things seem to be "too much"?

Please read Chapter 8.

1. Have you ever felt like you have heard God speak to you? Describe what was happening around you at the time.

2. When is the last time that you specifically came to God to just listen with no agenda of your own but to hear what He might have to say to you?

3. What gets in the way of making time to spend with God?

4. How important do you think it is to hear from God?

5. What are the two types of rest? Describe each in your own words.

6. What are the various ways that God can speak to people?

7. What are some things do you can do to help you hear from God?

8. What should you do if you've made the time to spend listening to God and you don't hear anything?

9. How does reading the Bible have anything to do with hearing from God?

10. Take a moment to outline how you spend each day. Make the time now to schedule a day in your calendar to spend with God. I promise it will be life-changing.

Memory Verse:

For the Lord gives wisdom, and from his mouth come knowledge and understanding. Proverbs 2:6

Still want a bit more?

Write down a verse you've read in the morning and keep it with you all day. Refer to it often. At the end of the day, look at it again and see if God has expanded the meaning by something that happened that day.

Faith Test
Chapter 9-Listen!
Questions

Questions to answer **before** you read:

Think of your last conversation. What was it about? Was there anything you heard that wasn't actually spoken with words?

What are the different ways that we listen?

How well do you think you listen? Ask someone you trust how well you listen?

Please read Chapter 9.

1. What does it mean that the Lord is one?

2. How does God speak in a circle in Deuteronomy 6:4-6?

3. Why does God occasionally speak in circles in the Bible?

4. What are the circles that the world teaches us?

5. Why does God value humility?

6. What commandments from God do you know off the top of your head?

7. When was the last time that you talked about God or His commands with someone?

8. What will help us to determine the will of God in our lives?

9. Think back about the times you felt closest to God or knew that He answered a prayer. See if you can make a list of these times.

10. List 10 things you are grateful for right now.

11. Define a "Living" sacrifice.

12. How can a person NOT belong to God's family?

13. Why does God want us to follow the example that Jesus set?

Memory Verse:
For the Lord gives wisdom, and from his mouth come knowledge and understanding. Proverbs 2:6

Still want a bit more?

In your next conversation with a family member or another believer, see if you can bring God into your conversation.

Start a journal of what you are learning when you read your Bible.

Faith Test
Chapter 10- Hearing from God
Questions

For this chapter, discuss your experience of hearing from God with others and be encouraged by asking others to share their experience of hearing God with you.

Memory Verse:

See, the former things have taken place, and new things I declare; before they spring into being I announce them to you. Isaiah 42:9

Notes:

Faith Test
Chapter 11- Healing
Questions

Questions to answer **before** you read:

Why do you think that Jesus healed people?

If a man in your neighborhood was teaching about God, would you go along? How about if he was healing people?

What are some things that you have tried to heal your body?

Please read Chapter Eleven

1. What is the mission of Jesus?

2. Why did Jesus tell the man with leprosy to go and show himself to the priests?

3. What is the purpose of a testimony?

4. What can Jesus give to you that is better than a physical healing?

5. Why did the Pharisees and the teachers of the law follow Jesus?

6. Who did Jesus heal?

7. In Luke 17:11-19, how many of the ten men who were healed of leprosy by Jesus came back to thank Him?

8. What have you recently thank God for?

9. Why could physical healing be detrimental to the soul?

10. When you are sick, what is the reasoning that goes through your mind?

11. What was the reason Jesus gave for the man being blind in John 9:1-3?

12. According to Paul in 2 Corinthians 12:7-10, why did God not heal him from the thorn in his flesh?

Memory Verse:

> To keep me from becoming conceited because of these surpassingly great revelations, there was given me a thorn in my flesh, a messenger of Satan, to torment me. Three times I pleaded with the Lord to take it away from me. But he said to me, "My grace is sufficient for you, for my power is made perfect in weakness."
>
> Therefore I will boast all the more gladly about my weaknesses so that Christ's power may rest on me. That is why, for Christ's sake, I delight in weaknesses, in insults, in hardships, in persecutions, in difficulties. For when I am weak then I am strong.
> 2 Corinthians 12:7-10

Still want to go deeper?

Look up some of the 300 prophesies from the Old Testament that were written so that people would know the Messiah when He came to earth.

Take your medical issue before God in prayer and let Him know that you are open to listening to whatever it is He wants to tell you.

Faith Test
Chapter 12- A Journey in Healing
Questions

For this chapter, discuss your experience of healing from God with others and be encouraged by asking others to share their experience of healing God with you.

Memory Verse:

Heal me, O Lord, and I will be healed; save me and I will be saved, for you are the one I praise." Jeremiah 17:14

Faith Test
Chapter 13- Grow up!
Questions

Questions to answer **before** you read:

What is something that you wish you could do over in your life?

How do you feel your life is different than other people's lives?

At what age did you appreciate your parents?

Please read Chapter Eleven

1. How are we meant to mature in faith with God?

2. How would you describe where you are on your journey of faith?

3. Describe the various types of relationship we have with God. Which do you feel you relate to God the most?

4. Describe a conflict that you have been through with an unnamed person from your past. How did you handle this conflict?

5. What is something an unnamed person from the church has done to hurt you in the past?

6. List the ways in which holding onto the hurt others have caused you can actually be harmful.

7. How can you change someone who is a source of conflict to you and others around you?

8. How can we prepare for conflict in the future?

9. With what type of person do you struggle to "do good"? What is a different way of seeing that person?

10. How should we handle conflict?

Memory Verse:

> "Therefore, as we have opportunity, let us do good to all people, especially to those who belong to the family of believers." Galatians 6:10

Still want to go deeper?

List some proverbs that will help you this week.

Write out 1 Corinthians 13 and replace the word 'love' with your name.

Faith Test
Chapter 14- Fear Factor
Questions

Questions to answer **before** you read:

What is something that you haven't done due to fear holding you back?

Describe how fear feels in different situations?

What was your very first fear? How did you deal with it?

Please read Chapter Eleven

1. Define fear.

2. Does it matter if one's fears are real or perceived?

3. What keeps fear alive in our lives?

4. Define the Fear of Man. How has this fear affected your life? What are some things that can help us overcome this fear?

5. Define the Fear of Failure. How has this fear affected your life? What are some things that can help us overcome this fear? Is God upset that you have fear?

6. Define the Fear of the Unknown. How has this fear affected your life? What are some things that can help us overcome this fear?

7. Define the Fear of Losing control. How has this fear affected your life? What do you like to control in your life? What are some things that can help us overcome this fear?

8. Define the Fear of evil. How has this fear affected your life? What types of things are you feeding your soul? What are some things that can help us overcome this fear?

9. Define the Fear of death. How has this fear affected your life? What are some things that can help us overcome this fear?

10. What are some things that you fear God might ask you to do? What is the worst thing that can happen? What is the best thing that can happen?

Memory Verse:

For God did not give us a spirit of timidity, but a spirit of power, of love and of self-discipline. 2 Timothy 1:7

Still want to go deeper?

Look up verses that specifically relate to fear. Write them down and start to say them when your fears pop up.

Talk to someone else about the fears you both face. Maybe you could pray together and help each other through those fears.

Faith Test
Chapter 15- It's not about the Money
Questions

Questions to answer **before** you read:

Have you ever donated money, time or given anything to a charity or organization?

Where does most of your money go after taxes?

Have you ever felt pressured to give money when you go to church? Explain.

What do you think the church does with the money it collects?

Please read Chapter Eleven

1. Who in your life inspires you in the way they give to others?

2. What is the best experience you have had in giving?

3. What is a tithe vs. an offering?

4. Why do you think that God asks us to give a portion of our money to the church?

5. Describe a time when you have been blessed by someone else's giving.

6. What are ways that people can rob others without technically committing a crime?

7. How can money actually ruin someone's life?

8. What's better than having riches?

9. Can a true Christian be rich?

10. How did Jesus handle his money?

11. How do you handle your money? What are some tips you have learned that you could share with others?

Memory Verse:

For God did not give us a spirit of timidity, but a spirit of power, of love and of self-discipline. 2 Timothy 1:7

Still want to go deeper?

Map out where you spend your time and money and ask God if you need to make some changes?

Pray to God about where He would want you to invest your money.

Research the charities you support to see how their money is spent.

Faith Test

Chapter 16- Can I get a Witness?
Questions

Questions to answer **before** you read:

What does the word "witness" mean to you?

Have you ever had someone "witness" to you? Describe the experience.

Please read Chapter Eleven

1. How are Christians a "witness" to the world around them?

2. Describe someone who has had a positive impact on your life?

3. What was your first experience of going to a church like?

4. Have you accepted Jesus as your Savior? Share how you came to that decision.

5. Describe a time when you talked about your spiritual beliefs with someone you didn't expect to.

6. What are some of the ways you have tried on someone else's "armor"?

7. Should we use tracts to tell others about Jesus?

8. Why is it important to talk with other Christians about what God is doing in our lives?

9. What does salvation mean?

10. What priority does prayer take in your life?

11. What do each of the pieces of armor symbolize?

Memory Verse:

> When the disciples heard this, they were greatly astonished and asked, "Who then can be saved?" Jesus looked at them and said, "With man this is impossible, but with God all things are possible." Matthew 19: 25-26

Still want to go deeper?

Make a list of people in your life and begin to pray for them.

Pray for someone for an hour and see where God leads.

Ark House Press
PO Box 1722, Port Orchard, WA 98366 USA
PO Box 1321, Mona Vale NSW 1660 Australia
PO Box 318 334, West Harbour, Auckland 0661 New Zealand
arkhousepress.com

© 2020 Marla Jones

All rights reserved. No part of this publication may be reproduced, stored in a retrieval system or transmitted in any form or by any means electronic, mechanical, photocopying, recording or otherwise without the prior written permission of the publisher.

All Scriptures are quoted from the New International Version (NIV) unless otherwise stated.

Cataloguing in Publication Data:
Title: Faith Test
ISBN: 978-0-6487607-9-5 (pbk.)
Subjects: Christian Living; Biography;
Other Authors/Contributors: Jones, Marla

Design and layout by initiateagency.com

www.ingramcontent.com/pod-product-compliance
Lightning Source LLC
LaVergne TN
LVHW051515070426
835507LV00023B/3118